POLISH WINGS 27

Marcin Wawrzynkowski

French Flying Boats 1924–1939

Lioré et Olivier LeO H-13B3, LeO H-13E,
CAMS 30E, Latham 43 HB.3,
Schreck FBA 17 HE.2,
Schreck FBA 17 HMT.2, Lioré et Olivier LeO H-135B3

STRATUS

Wydawnictwo STRATUS sp.j.
ul. Żeromskiego 4, 27-600 Sandomierz, Poland
phone. 0-15 833 30 41
e-mail: office@stratusbooks.pl
www.stratusbooks.com.pl www. mmpbooks.biz

ISBN 978-83-65958-50-1

PRINTED IN POLAND

The author would like to thank all the people and institutions involved for help with in the work on this publication for invaluable comments and making the photographs and documents available: Bartłomiej Belcarz, Janusz Światłoń, Mariusz Konarski, J. Fernandez, Joanna Grochowska, Barbara Kos-Dąbrowska, Andrzej Glass, Tomasz J. Kopański, Wiesław Bączkowski, Andrzej Morgała, Lechosław Musiałkowski, Wojtek Matusiak, Robert Gretzyngier, Jacek Dzienisiuk, Grzegorz Śliżewski, Władysław Szarski, Wiktor Kobylański, Renata Balewska, Marek Filzek, Wojciech Sokołowski, Coastal Defense Museum in Hel, Museum of the Puck Land, Naval Museum in Gdynia, Polish Aviation Museum in Kraków, National Digital Archive, Capital City of Warsaw Archives, National Library, Stratus Publishing. (The orignal names of the museums and archives can be found in the captions themselves).

Layout concept	Bartłomiej Belcarz
Cover concept	Artur Juszczak
Cover	Marcin Górecki
Translation	Tomasz Basarabowicz
Proofreading	Peter Brown
DTP	Bartłomiej Belcarz
Colour Drawings	Janusz Światłoń
Edited by	Roger Wallsgrove

ORGANIZATION OF POLISH NAVAL AVIATION

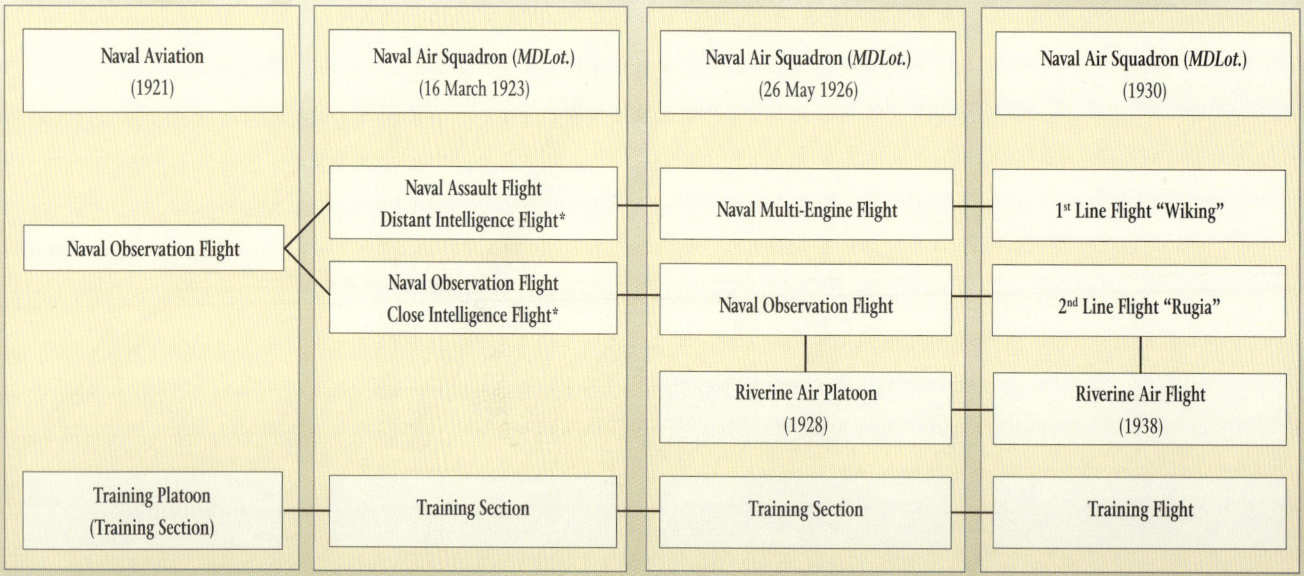

* Both the Distant Intelligence Flight and the Close Intelligence Flight in various documents are also called "Distant Intelligences Flight" or "Distant Reconnaissance and Bomber Flight", and "Close Intelligences Flight" as well as "Close Reconnaissance Flight". All of them should be treated as synonyms.

French aircraft in the Polish naval aviation

The Naval Air Squadron (*MDLot. – Morski Dywizjon Lotniczy*) stationed in Puck[1] was the only unit of maritime aviation in pre-war Poland. It was formed in 1911 at the site of the former German naval aviation base. It consisted of barracks, a grass runway 700 m long, four hangars and an 800-meter concrete pathway to transfer and taxi the seaplanes.

On 10 February 1920, near the aircraft hangars and at the exit of the aircraft slipway to the water, the historical ceremony of taking over Poland's coastline (called "nuptials" in Polish), celebrated by General Józef Haller took place, and on 1 July 1920, the Naval Air Base (*BLM – Baza Lotnictwa Morskiego*) in Puck was officially established as part of the Coastal Defence Command. In November 1921, the naval aviation was formed, having introduced the organizational division into the Sea Observation Squadron and the Air Training Platoon, later named the Exercise Section and the Base. The aircraft equipment was obtained in a semi-legal manner and slightly random way. These were German made hydroplanes, still of World War One vintage. The situation was to be improved by the purchase of nine Macchi M-9 flying boats and seven FBA S-4s from Italy. These were second-hand machines were in poor mechanical condition and after they had been delivered to Puck, it turned out that some of them (FBA S-4) were suitable only for scrapping, while the others (M-9) required a major overhaul, which was only started in 1923.

Organizationally, the naval aviation was subordinated to the 4th Department of Air Navigation of the Ministry of Military Affairs but remained subordinated to the Polish Navy which would cause constant equipment and financial problems. To improve the situation, the unit was removed from the naval establishment, and on 29 July 1922 it became a part the 2nd Air Regiment in Kraków as a Detached Air Scout Squadron with its Base in Puck. The unit was slowly losing its typically maritime character.

On 16 March 1923, an independent Naval Air Squadron (*MDLot.*) was formed. As far as equipment and personnel issues were concerned it was subordinated to the 4th Department of Air Navigation of the Ministry of Military Affairs, but in training and operational-tactical matters to the Naval and Coastal Services Command. Its new commander, observer Col. Antoni Leonkow was determined to depend solely on the Land Forces Command with independence from the Naval Command. The equipment situation was still not very good. German aircraft worn to their limits were still used, as well as the Italian M-9s which despite repairs and modernization were unreliable.

In 1924, an equipment and organisations revolution began at the Naval Air Squadron in Puck. On 20 April 1924 the Naval Directorate (*KMW – Kierownictwo Marynarki Wojennej*) presented another fleet expansion program, covering the period

1 Puck – a city in the so called Gdańsk Pomerania with 11,000 inhabitants. Upon getting access to the sea in 1920, it was the only port which Poland could use without any restrictions. Due to the location in the shallow waters of the Bay of Puck, it was not accessible to the merchant vessels, hence had no economic significance. Puck harbour was the first base of the Polish Navy.

[1]: Winter panorama of Puck as seen from the MDLot. *base. On the left, in the foreground, the warships moored in the port are visible, including one of the gunboats. On the right, the massive St. Peter and Paul Church. (NAC Archives)*

1.

2

[2]: *Nieuport Macchi M-9 flying boat on the apron of the Puck base. (Polish Aviation Museum Kraków coll.)*

of 1925–1928. It also contained the issue of naval aviation, despite the fact that it was not fully subjected to the *KMW*. The needs of this formation were understood and the necessity of its financial support was seen. While discussing the proposals of the plan to expand the fleet there was friction between the *KMW* and the 4th Department of Air Navigation, which in addition to budgetary problems, led ultimately to the cutting of expenditure on the development of the navy, and the funds allocated to the *MDLot.* were really small. In the Polish Navy budget amounting to 11 million zlotys in 1926, the unit at Puck received only 60,000 zlotys.

However, this did not prevent the search for modern aircraft. Offers began to stream in at the turn of 1923 and 1924. They came from British, Italian and French producers. Because the latter were considered one of the best at this time, it was them who received a large order for the supply of new flying equipment for Polish naval aviation. The order was placed in 1923 by the then head of the 4th Department of Air Navigation, a Frenchman, Gen. François-Léon Lévêque. Deliveries were to take place in 1924 as part of a loan granted by France to Poland for military purposes. In August 1924, the new head of the 4th Department of Air Navigation became Gen. Włodzimierz Zagórski-Ostoja. He made substantial purchases of aircraft in France not only for naval but also land-based aviation. A total of 40 flying boats were ordered for naval aviation, from four French factories: Latham, CAMS, Lioré et Olivier and FBA. Of the aircraft acquired, eight were long range patrol-attack machines and 16 were close range patrol aircraft, while the remaining 16 were training planes.

[3]: *The small port of Puck became the first base of the Polish Navy. The photograph depicts the first Polish warships – hydrographic ship ORP* Pomorzanin *(in the foreground at the quay) and the gunboats ORP* Komendant Piłsudski *(in the foreground) and ORP* Generał Haller *(in the background). On the horizon to the left, the village of Swarzewo is visible. On the right – the Hel Peninsula. (NAC Archive)*

3

[4]: Before the first French aircraft arrived in Puck, the basic flying equipment of the MDLot. *were the Italian flying boats Nieuport Macchi M-9. These were machines with good flight characteristics and performance, however, heavily worn out and unreliable despite major overhaul. (Bourdin family archive via J. Fernandez)*

[5]: A group of the MDLot. *officers pose for a photo at the post commemorating Poland's takeover of the coastline. The fifth from the left is the commander of the* MDLot.*, Col. Antoni Leonkow. (MOW in Hel collection)*

[6]: Maj. Gen. Włodzimierz Zagórski-Ostoja in flying overalls, posing for pictures with the Breguet 19 aircraft. As the commander of aviation he continued the policy of substantial purchases of aircraft from France, including flying boats. (NAC Archive)

[7]: Panorama of Puck from a bird's eye view. In the upper part of the photo, the MDLot. *base is clearly visible with its entire infrastructure, apron, hangars and the system of small docks. (MOW in Hel coll.)*

[8]: The first modern flying boats reached Puck on board the ORP Warta *transport. (NAC Archive)*

[9]: The transport ORP Wilia *which also carried war materiel for Poland, including other flying boats to Puck. (MOW in Hel coll.)*

10

[10]: The first of the LeO H-13B3 flying boats delivered to Poland, in front of which a group of officers of the unit poses. In the centre, 9th from the left, the unit commanding officer observer Col. Antoni Leonkow is standing. He strived to subordinate the unit to land-based aviation and become independent of the Naval Command. This can be confirmed even by the uniforms worn by the officers visible in the photograph. (Bourdin family archive via J. Fernandez)

11

[11]: A group of pilots poses against one of the flying boats LeO H-13B. The first from the left is pilot Lt. Adolf Stempkowski. In a leather coat and flying helmet is Lucien Borduin, the French factory pilot who supervised the introduction of new flying boats into service. (Bourdin family archive via J. Fernandez)

[12]: The LeO H-13B3 flying boat No. 1-2 is being pulled onto the apron in Puck. The picture was taken most probably in 1924–1925 as evidenced by the black anchor painted on the bow and the aircraft number. The Polish chequerboards on the lower surfaces of the wings and stabilizer are painted with the correct layout of white and red squares. (Bourdin family archive via J. Fernandez)

12

13

[13]: Introduction into service of the new French machines was widely commented on in the local press. No wonder that the large flying boats were eagerly watched by the inhabitants of Puck and holiday-makers resting on the seaside. In the picture, the LeO H-13B flying boat No. 1-2 at one of the beaches in Puck. (Bourdin family archive via J. Fernandez)

14

[14]: LeO H-13B flying boat in the air! "Flights of huge seaplanes. Puck. On the 16th of the current month there were trial flights of huge seaplanes of the French type at the local naval aviation base. The flights were performed by the French instructor de Bourdeu (Lucien Bourdin – Author) who came from France and whose task will also be to train all pilots on the said seaplanes. The seaplanes were brought a dozen or so weeks ago by the transport ORP Warta. *Trial flights demonstrated their great efficiency. Hydroplanes have two motors with an output of 150 horsepower".* ("Słowo Pomorskie", 10.05.1925, Issue No. 117). *(Bourdin family archive via J. Fernandez)*

15

[15]: Lucien Borduin (seen on the right) watching the setting of the flying boat LeO H-13B No. 1-1 on the water by the Puck base personnel. (Bourdin family archive via J. Fernandez)

Due to these orders and their implementation, the *MDLot.* in Puck was to become a powerful fully-fledged first-line unit with modern machines.

In November 1924, the first modern flying boat, a Lioré et Olivier LeO H-13B3, was delivered to Puck by the transport ship ORP *Warta*. The second machine of this type reached Puck by rail on 19 January 1925. At this time, two more aircraft of the E variant arrived in Puck, which were to be used for training purposes. They were assembled and flown in March 1925 by Lucien Bourdin, a factory pilot of the Lioré et Olivier company, who then trained the *MDLot.* pilots and for several years he stayed in Puck as an instructor. Because his contributions to the development of Polish naval aviation are invaluable, it is worth devoting a bit more attention to him here[2].

Lucien Bourdin arrived in Puck together with the first LeO H-13B3 flying boats, which took place at the turn of 1924 and 1925. His main task was to supervise their assembly carried out by *MDLot.* workshops, and then test flying and training of Polish sea airmen on the new equipment. Bourdin was a complete opposite to the Italians, who also were staying in Puck – pilot Adolfo Frigierio and mechanic Vittorio Prodolini. They were to supervise the assembly, to test fly and train on Nieuport Macchi M-9 flying boats, and after having spent a year in Puck, they stated that they would not fly these aircraft, and as a result, were removed from the unit's facilities. The Frenchman performed his new duties with great commitment, gaining great affection among pilots and mechanics. *"After a day of flights, he was going with Polish pilots for a drink*

2 Lucien Bourdin was born on 5 August 1896 in Romorantin (Loir-et-Cher). He was one of the most outstanding French test pilots of the interwar period. For the entire period of his career he was associated with the Lioré et Oliver company. Initially, he worked as a test pilot, and eventually became the company's head pilot. He established many international records for seaplanes, mainly flying boats. He took part in experimental work on the development of LeO H-255 aircraft, the Leo H-46 torpedo-bomber aircraft, and finally the four-engine flying boat LeO H-47 intended for transatlantic flights. Lucien Bourdin died with the majority of the crew in a plane crash on 19 May 1937 when, on the coast of the Antibes (Alpes-Maritimes), the LeO H-47 flying boat called "Atlantique-1" and licensed F-APPR piloted by himself, crashed. The plane hit the sea immediately after take-off and caught fire. Apart from Bourdin, four members of the crew of ten perished. This catastrophe was a great tragedy for the entire French air community. Lucien Borduin's body was never found, most likely he drowned in the sea.

16

[16]: Lucien Bourdin was the test pilot of the Lioré et Olivier plant. In Puck, he was to supervise the assembly of LeO H-13 aircraft, and then train Polish pilots on them. In the picture (second from the left) he can be seen along with a group of pilots in front of the Naval Observation Flight's HQ building, colloquially called the "Pilots' House". (Bourdin family archive via J. Fernandez)

of vodka, and he did not bring shame to France"[3]. Before Lucien Bourdin was recognised as a good companion, he had demonstrated that he was a great pilot and a demanding instructor. The new flying boats were used in parallel with the upgraded M-9. In 1926–1927, 37 more seaplanes were delivered to Puck from France, including eight Latham 43 HB.3 heavy reconnaissance and bombing flying boats, four CAMS 30E training and reconnaissance flying boats, six Schreck FBA 17 HE.2 training and liaison flying boats and 12 Schreck FBA 17 HMT.2 liaison flying boats plus seven LeO H-135B3 reconnaissance flying boats.

Acquisition of modern flying equipment gave rise to the need to modernize the base itself, in order to adapt it for servicing of new aircraft. The runway itself had been rebuilt, its technical facilities had been significantly expanded. This applied, in particular, to the network of small docks intended for stationing the seaplanes as well as the floating equipment used in the base. In total, there were now five such docks (at the time of taking over the base from German hands there were just two), but the most visible element of the modernization of the base was a special crane for lifting seaplanes and setting them on the water. It had a steel, openwork construction, and it was placed on three concrete pedestals at one of the berths. Thanks to the crane, it was possible to safely manoeuvre a suspended seaplane on a circle with a diameter of 60 meters. The crane was mainly used to operate Latham 43 HB.3 heavy flying boats. The aircraft were delivered to Puck in large wooden

3 Andrzej Celarek: *Morski Dywizjon Lotniczy. Wspomnienia pilotów*, Wyd. DJ, Gdańsk 2002, p. 60.

[17]: Lucien Bourdin together with a group of pilots of the Naval Air Squadron. (Bourdin family archive via J. Fernandez)

[18]: A typical bustle in the base while servicing airplanes. In the background a LeO H-13 flying boat. (Bourdin family archives via J. Fernandez)

19

[19]: Before the next training flight. Lucien Bourdin (in the flying overalls) in conversation with a group of the MDLot. officers. (Bourdin family archive via J. Fernandez)

20

[20]: The summer was really warm that year. The flying boat LeO H-13E 1-4 on the slipway of the Naval Air Squadron base in Puck. Note non-standard marking pattern – a Polish chequerboard painted much higher than on other aircraft, and individual black numbering N:14 without a dash. The photograph was taken most likely before 1927, when a new camouflage pattern was introduced. (MOW in Hel coll.)

[21]: The new planes were the sensation wherever they appeared. The flying boat LeO H-13E No. 1-4 is admired by holiday-makers at the beach in Gdynia. (Bourdin family archive via J. Fernandez)

21

[22]: A commemorative photograph of officer cadets of the 1906 age-group with an unpopular plane in the background – a CAMS 30E flying boat. (MOW in Hel coll.)

[23]: In 1927 a group of the US Navy officers visited Puck. First on the right pilot Lt. Adolf Stempkowski, in the background the Schreck FBA 17 HE.2 flying boat on the slipway. (Muzeum Ziemi Puckiej Archives)

crates. Use was quickly found for the large number of planks left from the crates. A barrack accommodating the officers' mess was built from them, which survived until the outbreak of World War Two.

As part of the *MDLot.*, in 1926 the following sub-units were formed: the 1st Naval Observation Flight (six Schreck FBA 17 HE.2/HMT.2s and two machines of this type in reserve), the 2nd Naval Assault Flight (six Latham 43 HB.3s and two in reserve) and the Training Section (two each of LeO H-13B3, CAMS 30E, Schreck FBA 17 HE.2 and two each of LeO H-13E and CAMS 30E, Schreck FBA 17 HE.2 in reserve). According to the order of the commander of the unit on 31 May 1926, the assignment of eight aircraft per flight and the principle of equipment circulation were introduced. It was about maintaining a full-time personnel establishment in individual flight, while the planes were to be changed cyclically and subjected to repairs, maintenance or moved to reserve to replace those that had already flown out their flight cycle between repairs. In the year in which the rules described above were introduced, 18 aircraft were in current use and 14 machines in reserve, which gave a total of 32 seaplanes. A year later, this amount increased to 42 aircraft with the arrival of seven LeO H-135B3 flying boats and the introduction of three liaison aircraft on wheeled undercarriage.

In February 1927, there was a change in the position of the commander of the unit. The new *MDLot.'s* commander became pilot-observer Lt.-Cmdr. Karol Trzasko-Durski and with him began the period of systematic return of *MDLot.* to the naval establishment. The unit regained its original maritime character. It was re-formed in 1928 and from then on consisted of the Multi-Engine Naval Flight, Naval Observation Flight, Training Section, Naval Aviation Ordnance Park, HQ Section, Harbour Detachment, Radio-Technical Section and Photographic Section.

In May 1928 a small air sub-unit was detached from *MDLot.* and sent to Pińsk in Polesie. Since only *MDLot.* had equipment suitable for operations in the specific conditions of the River Pripyat basin, it was responsible for forming a riverine platoon. After appropriate tests and exercises, for which a LeO H-13E flying boat was used, the usefulness of the air unit in the Pińsk Riverine Flotilla had been proven, which is why the Riverine Air Platoon (*RPL – Rzeczny Pluton Lotniczy*) was established, which took place on 10 May 1928. It consisted of three Schreck FBA 17 HMT.2 flying boats, and its task was to conduct reconnaissance and fire control of the riverine boats' guns. The platoon consisted of 24 officers, NCOs and other ranks.

The modernized base in Puck became, over time, a showcase of the town and the centre of its life. It was also a place of fre-

[24]: In front of the "Black Hall" of the Puck base. On the apron from the left CAMS 30E floatplane No. 2-3, amphibious plane Schreck FBA 17 HMT.2 and flying boat FBA 17 HE.2. It is worth noting the different types of windshields used in the HMT.2 and HE.2 versions. The French manufacturer did not apply itself to paint the chequerboards. On the wings, there is the correct layout of colours, on the stabilizer – there is not. Reduced lighting makes it impossible to identify both machines by numbers. In the hangar, part of a LeO H. flying boat is visible. (Muzeum Marynarki Wojennej in Gdynia Archives)

24

25

[25]: Latham 43 HB.3 heavy flying boat No. 3-2 being set on the water with the crane. In the foreground, a wooden wheeled cart is visible which was used for moving the plane. (Tomasz Kopański coll.)

[26]: The Latham 43 HB.3 heavy flying boat lifted from the water with the crane. The plane sports the overall light grey-blue camouflage pattern, clearly visible are the chequerboards painted on the horizontal rudder planes. (MOW in Hel coll.)

26

quent visits by naval airmen from other countries. The *MDLot.* hosted, inter alia, Italian, English, Danish and German pilots as well as crews from other countries. Polish pilots also visited their foreign colleagues in, among others, Copenhagen and Liepaja. There were also a number of long-distance flights across the country, including to Kraków, Warsaw, Toruń and Poznań.

In 1930, changes were made to the organization of the unit. From this year on the *MDLot.* consisted of the 1st Line Flight "Wiking", 2nd Line Flight "Rugia", Training Flight, Harbour Detachment, Meteorological Section, and Quartermaster. However, the beginning of the 1930s brought in another equipment crisis. The French-made planes, the life cycle of which was calculated as five years, were already largely worn out. There were frequent accidents and crashes. The reason was usually the deteriorating technical condition of the flying equipment. The engines were failing, the fuselage structures did not withstand the passing of time. The French planes were gradually withdrawn from active service. They were replaced with Lublin R-VIIIter/hydro and Lublin R-XIIIter/hydro patrol floatplanes as well as Lublin G/hydro, however this was treated as a stop-gap solution, until the introduction of modern torpedo-bomber seaplanes from both imports and domestic manufacturers. These plans, however, were not implemented due to the outbreak of World War Two. The Naval Air Squadron in Puck had to enter the war with outdated and worthless combat equipment, among which there were two flying boats recalling the best years of the Puck's unit, Schreck FBA 17 HE.2s.

[27]: The Multi-Engine Flight personnel pose for a commemorative photograph with the LeO H-135B3 amphibious plane No. 61. Seated fifth from the left in the bottom row is pilot Lt. Adolf Stempkowski. The rounded building visible in the background accommodated the Wireless Section and Quality Control. (Muzeum Ziemi Puckiej coll.)

[28]: In front of the Wireless Section and Quality Control building. One of numerous commemorative photographs. The Leo H-135B3 No. 61 of the Multi-Engine Flight can be seen. (MOW in Hel coll.)

Camouflage and Markings

For a number of years, there have been a variety of theories and even speculations on the subject of the schemes of painting and marking of seaplanes of French production used in the Polish naval aviation. Until now, knowledge on this subject, based mainly on period black and white photographs, allows for some systematisation. The pictorial material examined so far indicates in almost unambiguous manner that all types of French aircraft throughout their period of service retained their factory painting schemes, therefore according to the standards used in the French naval aviation. Throughout the period of service, the aircraft underwent periodic repairs, during which the wooden planking as well as canvas skin were replaced, which necessitated the renewal of the paint as well. Also during these operations aircraft retained their previous painting schemes. The situation also did not change from the time of the entry into service of domestic production aircraft, i.e. Lublin R-VIII ter/G and Lublin R-XIII ter/G, which were painted according to a completely different scheme. The last remaining French-made planes, two amphibious Schreck FBA 17 HMT.2 aircraft, also at the outbreak of the war, sported the French camouflage pattern.

The first machines supplied from France were four flying boats – two LeO H-13B3s and two LeO H-13Es. The preserved images allow for the exact reproduction of their painting scheme. It was the standard camouflage applied in French naval aviation. The upper part of the fuselage and the fuel tank on the upper plane were painted in grey-blue (*Gris Bleu Foncé*), while the lateral surfaces of the fuselage, upper and lower surfaces of the wings and horizontal rudder were light blue (*Gris Bleu Clair*). The engine nacelles were left in natural metal colour (aluminium). The LeO H-135B3 amphibious aircraft were painted the same way. Most probably in 1926, the painting scheme of both LeO H-13E training flying boats was changed. All upper and lateral surfaces are painted in grey-blue (*Gris Bleu Foncé*) with the bottom surfaces in light grey-blue (*Gris Bleu Clair*). The largest group of aircraft delivered to Puck from France were Schreck FBA 17 HE.2 flying boats and Schreck FBA 17 HMT.2 amphibious planes. Also in the case of these machines, a lot of pictures have been found to date which allows for a fairly accurate reproduction of their painting scheme. The upper surfaces of the elevators and wings as well as the upper surfaces of the fuselages and the stabilizer were covered with blue-grey paint (*Gris Bleu Foncé*). Bottom wing surfaces, elevators, fuselage side areas and also the vertical rudder were painted light grey-blue (*Gris Bleu Clair*). The fuselages below the waterline were covered with a protective

29

[29]: Flying boat LeO H-13B No. 1-2 when casting (or maybe weighing?) its anchor. Clearly visible are the details of camouflage and markings as well as the fan driving the generator. The chequerboard on the lower surface of the wing is painted correctly. (Bourdin family archive via J. Fernandez)

30

[30]: The crew in their seats, the engines are working, you can start. The LeO H-13B flying boat 1-2 just before taking off from the waters of the Bay of Puck. The details of the aircraft's construction are clearly visible. (Bourdin family archive via J. Fernandez)

[31]: The seaplanes were flown much and often. The photograph depicts the preparations for the launch of both LeO H-13E flying boats for a joint take-off. Unfortunately, the quality of the picture does not allow us to determine which boat is already on the water and which will be set on it. (Bourdin family archive via J. Fernandez)

31

32

[32]: The LeO H-13E No. 1-4 passing over Gdynia. The aircraft has an anchor painted at the bow and a black No. 4 which proves that the picture was taken in the first half of the 1920s. The chequerboards on the top surfaces of the wings are painted with an inverted layout of squares. It is worth noting that visible on the left side of the picture is the villa district of Kamienna Góra together with the modern hotel "Polska Riviera" and the beach. On the right side, you can see the buildings of the village of Gdynia along with the road and the railway line leading to Gdańsk. (Muzeum Ziemi Puckiej coll.)

[33]: The LeO H-135B3 amphibious aircraft Nos. 61 and 65 during engine start-up in winter. Both machines have their chequerboards correctly painted only on the lower surfaces of the wings, on vertical stabilizers they were painted with an inverted layout of squares. (MOW in Hel coll.)

33

34

[34]: One of many commemorative photos. Non-commissioned officers against the LeO H-135B3 amphibious aircraft. Clearly visible is the emblem of the 2nd Line Flight "Rugia"(Wiesław Bączkowski archives from Stratus coll.)

coating against the harmful effects of seawater. The coating was of black (*Noir*) colour.

The least numerous type of French seaplanes used in the Naval Air Squadron were the CAMS 30E training flying boats. These machines were painted according to the following pattern: blue-grey (*Gris Bleu Foncé*) on all upper and side surfaces, lower surfaces of wings and horizontal rudder in light grey (*Gris Clair*), fuselage to the waterline with black (*Noir*) coating.

The issue of the painting scheme applied on the largest machines of French production used at Puck, that is, Latham 43 HB.3 heavy flying boats, looked slightly different. The upper and side surfaces of these aircraft were painted light grey-blue (*Gris Bleu Clair*), while the bottom ones were light grey (*Gris Clair*). Part of the components of all aircraft types were left in the natural finish of the material from which they were made. These were engine nacelles, which in the case of LeO H aircraft in all variants and Latham 43 HB.3 were of aluminium colour, all kinds of fittings, handles or machine gun mounts, were of steel colour. The propellers were stained wood colour.

Over the years, there have been many anecdotal theories on the camouflage pattern of all French aircraft used in *MDLot*. There were speculations on the existence of more or less significant deviations from the original factory painting, which were to be attained on the occasion of repairs and repainting of individual aircraft. It has been speculated, for example, that the lower surfaces of the LeO H-13B3s and LeO H-13Es were painted in silver grey, while olive-coloured paint covered the side surfaces of the fuselage and the upper surfaces of the wings and the tail planes. There were also hypotheses about the fact that the CAMS 30E and Latham 43 HB.3 flying boats, after major refurbishment, were to receive the colours like grey-green, olive-green, khaki or sea grey-green, corresponding to the Lublin R-VIII and R-XIII aircraft which were entering service. Regarding the Latham 43 HB.3, there is also the theory that

one airplane of this type was painted in overall black. However, did these changes of shades and colours of individual aircraft actually take place? Or was it just the effect of lighting conditions and the camera setting while taking pictures? There is no unambiguous answer to this question.

Aircraft intended for Poland were painted with the national markings or chequerboards in French factories. At first glance, the French producers showed a freedom in this respect bordering on nonchalance, completely ignoring the Polish regulations on the markings of military aircraft. According to the latter in force in 1925–1926, the chequerboards were to be applied on both sides of the vertical rudder, on the top surfaces of the upper wing, and on the lower surfaces of the lower wing. The chequerboards were painted in a symmetrical way. French manufacturers applied the chequerboards in accordance with these guidelines, and even went a little further, because on the CAMS 30E and Latham 43 HB.3 aircraft the chequerboards were also painted on the lower and upper surfaces of the horizontal tail-planes. In many cases chequerboards were painted with an inverted layout of squares, i.e. the left upper square was white and not red (magenta) as required by Polish regulations. Interestingly, only a part of the markings was painted in this way. The most vivid example is the way of painting chequerboards on the Latham 43 HB.3 heavy flying boats. Aeroplane No. 3-2 had its markings on the stabilizer and on the lower surfaces of the wings painted correctly, but on the top surfaces of the wings they were applied the wrong way. Chequerboards with an inverted layout of squares on the vertical stabilizers were painted on planes Nos. 3-1, 3-5 and 3-7. In a slightly more orderly way they were painted on Schreck FBA 17 HE.2 flying boats and Schreck FBA 17 HMT.2 amphibious planes. In the correct way, the chequerboards were painted only on the lower surfaces of the lower wing, while the remaining national markings had an inverted layout of squares. The CAMS-30E aircraft, in turn, had all chequerboards painted with an inverted square layout. The first two French planes delivered to Puck, i.e. the LeO H-13B3 and LeO H-13E flying boats, had their chequerboards painted in the correct way on the lower surfaces of the lower plane. The manner of painting the national identity markings on the stabilizer was completely different. The preserved images indicates that on the left side of the horizontal rudder there were chequerboards painted correctly, and on the right with an inverted layout of squares. The chequerboard on the port side was a mirror image of the starboard one, which was not a question of arbitrariness or chance. Interestingly, upon delivery to Puck, at least one of these aircraft, No. 1-2, did not have a chequerboard on the upper surfaces of the upper wing. The other planes had the chequerboards on the top surfaces of the upper wing painted with an inverted layout of squares. All LeO H-135B3 aircraft

35

[35]: A nose part of the LeO H-135B3 amphibious aircraft from the 2nd Line Flight "Rugia". Clearly visible is the squadron emblem and details such as a turntable with a machine gun and a generator for powering the wireless set. (Wojtek Matusiak coll.)

36

[36]: The Bay of Puck in 1930. Anchored flying boats were a frequent sight for those walking along the shoreline. In the foreground LeO H-135B3 amphibious aircraft No. 3 from the 2nd Line Flight "Rugia", followed by three Latham 43 HB.3 heavy flying boats from the 1st Line Flight "Wiking". Note the flight insignia painted on the noses of the aircraft. (Muzeum Ziemi Puckiej coll.)

had chequerboards painted in the same way. It is not really known why the Polish national markings were so painted. It should be noted that aircraft of naval aviation were no exception. On other aircraft purchased in France the chequerboards were painted the same way. Therefore, it is difficult to answer today whether it resulted from the difference between the heraldic rules in France and ordinary negligence. Interestingly, during their period of service with the Naval Air Squadron, the airplanes were repainted, but the chequerboards retained their original layout. Whereas when in 1926 the camouflage and marking pattern of both LeO H-13E aircraft was changed, huge chequerboards in the nose part of the fuselage were also painted with an inverted arrangement of squares. Why? At the moment, we do not know...

All aircraft ordered in France were delivered to Puck without numerical markings. Only on the stabilizer above the chequerboard there was an inscription informing about the type of the aircraft and its individual number, but it should be presumed that the latter was painted upon arrival in Poland, after an airplane had found itself in the unit records. Below the anchor there was a set of weight markings. The arrangement of these varied slightly depending on the type of aircraft. The Latham 43 HB.3 flying boats still had a painted anchor overlapping the chequerboard. The inscriptions on the rudder were painted in black, except for the CAMS 30E aircraft, where the inscriptions were white.

Numeric markings took various forms depending on the period of service. The first four LeO H-13B3/E flying boats were marked with black anchors, modelled on French insignia as well as black numbers. The LeO H-13B3s were allocated the numbers 1 and 2, while LeO H-13Es had numbers 3 and 4. These markings were painted in the nose part of the fuselage on the left side. In 1926 the markings of both LeO H-13E flying boats were changed. Black numbers were replaced with white ones painted in

37

[37]: A group of holiday-makers posing for a commemorative photo at flying boat Schreck FBA 17 HE.2 No. 4? The lady on the left rather did not realize that in 80 years someone will wonder what number the airplane had... (MOW in Hel coll.)

[38]: The beach in Hel, 1929. Those wonderful men and their wonderful machines! Which of you ladies would not like a photo with MDLot. *pilots and their airplane? Who is this lady in the picture is unknown. On the other hand it is known, that the officer on the left is Lt. Pil. Adolf Stempkowski and in the background flying boat FBA 17 HE.2 No. 42. (Muzeum Ziemi Puckiej coll.)*

38

[39]: 7 May 1930, "Poniatówka" beach in Warsaw, L.O.P.P. Week. The Latham 43 HB.3 flying boat No. 34, moored at the beach, was part of the 1st Line Flight "Wiking", its emblem can be seen on the nose of the airplane. No large numbers on the fuselage, a small number along with other inscriptions were placed on the stabilizer. Attention should be paid to the covers over the machine gun positions, cockpit and engines. In the background, the Poniatowski Bridge is visible. (NAC Archive)

[40]: The rear part of the fuselage and the tail of the Latham 43 HB.3 No. 3-3. Clearly visible are the chequerboards on a horizontal rudder, as well as explanatory and weight inscriptions. The picture was taken on the beach in Oksywie, on the right side the stern of a cruiser is visible. It is the ORP Bałtyk *hulk ship. (Wojtek Matusiak coll.)*

[41]: The Schreck FBA 17 HE.2 No. 4-4 flying boat taking off. The windscreen adapted from the Schreck FBA 17 HMT.2 can clearly be seen. (Tomasz J. Kopański coll.)

the middle part of the fuselage. Also in the case of LeO H-13B3 aircraft, the marking pattern changed, it happened in 1930 when these airplanes were incorporated into the *MDLot.'s* Training Section. The black numbers on the port side were replaced by white numbering, painted in the middle of the fuselage. On the fuselage nose, the Section insignia was painted on both sides. All other types of aircraft imported from France were marked using a two-digit system that would survive until the outbreak of World War Two. The first number indicated the type of the machine, the second one was its individual number.

The Naval Air Squadron's numerical markings system

LeO H-13B3	LeO H-13E	CAMS 30E	Latham 43 HB.3	Schreck FBA 17 HE.2	Schreck FBA 17 HMT.2	LeO H-135B3
1-1	1-3	2-1, 21	3-1, 31	4-1, 41	5-1, 51	6-1, 61
1-2	1-4	2-2, 22	3-2, 32	4-2, 42	5-2, 52	6-2, 62
		2-3, 23	3-3, 33	4-3, 43	5-3, 53	6-3, 63
		2-4, 24	3-4, 34	4-4, 44	5-4, 54	6-4, 64
			3-5, 35	4-5, 45	5-5, 55	6-5, 65
			3-6, 36	4-6, 46	5-6, 56	6-6, 66
			3-7, 37		5-7, 57	6-7, 67
			3-8, 38		5-8, 58	
					5-9, 59	
					5-0, 50	
					Lubliniak, 511	
					L.O.P.P., 512	

These numbers were placed in the nose part of the aircraft, on both sides. At the beginning, both digits were separated by a dash, which was discontinued after periodic repairs carried out in the later period, with numbers on Latham 43 HB.3 flying boats painted much less carefully than on the other types. In the case of Latham 43 HB.3 aircraft, it should also be noted that before the above-mentioned marking system was introduced, these airplanes on the left side of the nose part were marked with a small black lettering with type of aircraft and the number: "Latham No. 5" for instance. In 1930 two-digit numbers were replaced with a single digit, painted in the middle of the fuselage. However, this applied only to aircraft incorporated into the 1st Line Flight "Wiking", the 2nd Line Flight "Rugia" and the Training Section, but not even all of them. The remaining planes, that is part of the Schreck FBA 17 HE.2/HMT.2 machines and all CAMS 30Es, retained their previous markings. Both civilian Schreck FBA 17 HMT.2 amphibious aircraft after their takeover by the *MDLot.* in the early 1930s, were allocated numbers 511 (ex – "Lubliniak") and 512 (ex – "L.O.P.P"). These numbers, painted white, were placed on the nose part of both airplanes on both sides. In August 1939 the last change in the method of numerical marking in the Naval Air Squadron in Puck took place. Large white digits were replaced with black ones of much smaller size. This was also true for both remaining Schreck FBA 17 HE.2 Nos. 42 and 44 flying boats. Until now, it remains a mystery why one of these machines changed its designation to 40, although the numerical system

42

[42]: The Schreck FBA 17 HE.2 flying boat No. 40 (4-0) photographed near the naval port in Hel. In the background behind the breakwater is the submarine ORP Wilk. *The photograph was taken in August 1939. At that time there was a change in the method of painting numbers, white large digits were replaced by much smaller black digits. The colour separation lines are visible in the photo before the windshield and on the waterline denote that the original French camouflage pattern had been preserved. In the middle is Mate Jerzy Dzienisiuk. (Jacek Dzienisiuk coll.)*

43

[43]: The Schreck FBA 17 HMT.2 amphibious aircraft No. 52 photographed at the base in Puck. The number of the aircraft is without a dash between digits. Also noteworthy is the absence of under-wing floats. (Lechosław Musiałkowski coll.)

used in the Naval Air Squadron allocated such a number for the tenth consecutive machine of a given type, and of the Schreck FBA 17 HE.2 flying boats there were six, as we remember. Some of the aircraft supplied to Poland had factory markings in the form of manufacturers' logos. They were usually painted in the nose part of airplanes. All types of the CAMS 30E Nos. 2-4 flying boats and Schreck FBA 17 HMT.2 "Lubliniak" were marked in this way. The logo was a pennant in the national colours of France with black FBA letters, it was modified to single-colour, most likely in order to eliminate the colours of a foreign state.

Three of the French seaplanes delivered to Poland were decorated with occasional markings. These were two civilian Schreck FBA 17 HMT.2 amphibious aircraft, the abovementioned "Lubliniak" and "L.O.P.P". Inscriptions in a light colour (most likely white) were placed on the nose part of both planes, on both sides. The inscription *Lubliniak czytelników Głosu Lubelskiego* ("Lublin readers of Głos Lubelski newspaper") was painted most probably in the winter of 1926 at the airfield in Lublin. At that time, the machine was offered to L.O.P.P. ("Anti-Aircraft and Anti-Gas League") in the presence of the Lublin governor, S. Bryla, godparents of the plane and invited guests. However, there is no unambiguous data, where the foundation inscriptions on the second civilian Schreck FBA 17 HMT.2 – "L.O.P.P" were painted. It is known that these inscriptions were made after the airplane had been delivered

[44]: 15 July of each year was celebrated in MDLot. *as the Unit's Day. In this photograph taken after 1926 there are two Schreck FBA 17 HE.2 flying boats, probably before or after the display flight for the audience gathered at the base. The flying boat visible in the background of the picture sports the number 44 or 41, while the way the photograph was taken makes it impossible to read the number of the flying boat in the foreground. In the background there is the port of Puck and the St. Peter and Paul Church. (Muzeum Ziemi Puckiej coll.)*

44

to Poland, but it is not known whether they were painted in Puck, Warsaw or elsewhere. The painting of foundation inscriptions on both aircraft necessitated repainting the fuselages of both machines. In the case of "Lubliniak" the waterline had an uneven, wavy contour at the place where the inscription was placed, while in the case of "L.O.P.P." the fuselage sides were covered entirely with blue-grey (*Gris Bleu Foncé*) colour. The third airplane, on which the occasional sign was placed, was the CAMS 30E flying boat No. 2-2. This painting was created after the machine was withdrawn from active service, and the occasion was the 8th Week L.O.P.P., 5-12 July 1931. A special inscription was placed on the fuselage "*VIII. tydzień L.O.P.P. 5/VII – 12/VII*" painted at the base in Puck, most likely in white. At the moment, one picture is known which does not allow to determine whether the inscription was placed on both sides of the fuselage or on starboard only.

Along the change of the organizational structure of the *MDLot.*, carried out in 1930, on the machines incorporated into the 1st Line Flight "Wiking", the 2nd Line Flight "Rugia" and the Training Sections, sometimes called Flight as well, the colourful insignia of these sub-units were displayed. All of them were in the form of circles with colourful graphic elements. The preserved iconography demonstrates precisely how elements of these emblems were composed, while their colours can only be the subject of deduction. Individual colours are more or less presumed. It should be assumed that they were kept in line with the colours associated with the sea, therefore various shades of blue and green. The insignia of the 1st Line Flight "Wiking" was the head of the dragon, referring to figures decorating the stems of *drekkars* – Viking boats. The emblem of the 2nd Line Flight "Rugia" was the image of *Światowid*, a Slavic deity with four faces looking at the four sides of the world. The insignia of the Training Flight was in turn a question mark placed over the sea waves. Other markings were also used in the form of dark (probably red) vertical stripes painted in the tail section of planes. Photographs exist of the heavy flying boats Latham 43 HB.3 and Schreck FBA 17 HMT.2 amphibious aircraft sporting such markings. What their purpose was is still a mystery.

45 *[45]: Exiled in Polesie... The Schreck FBA 17 HMT.2 amphibious aircraft No. 53 somewhere on the Pina River floodwaters. (MOW in Hel coll.)*

[46]: The base of the Naval Air Squadron in Puck. On the apron there are two Schreck FBA 17 HE.2 flying boats Nos. 41 and 45 (late variant of marking), in the waters of the Bay of Puck there are two Latham 43 HB.3 heavy assault flying boats prepared for take-off. In the background, the Hel Peninsula is visible. It is also worth paying attention to the equipment for servicing aircraft. Linz motorboats are visible in a small harbour basin, and the wheeled carts for rolling the Latham 43 HB.3 flying boats are on the right. (MOW in Hel coll.)

46

Lioré et Olivier LeO H-13B3 & LeO H-13E

The first LeO H-13B3 flying boats which were delivered to Puck were used for close reconnaissance, bombing and training. These were two-engine machines with a wooden structure and a biplane arrangement. A truss-shaped hull covered with plywood, flat bottom with step and three open crew cockpits connected by a communication shaft inside, along the axis of the fuselage. The main difference between the H-13B3 and H-13E versions was the location of the pilots' cockpit. In the first case, it was directly behind the wings' central part. The pilot was on the left and the observer on the right. In the case of training machines, the H-13E pilots' cabin was placed in front of the wings. The wings were of wooden construction, covered with canvas and of the rectangular planform.

The first of these aircraft was delivered to Puck in November 1924 and the second one in January 1925. These were flying boats of the H-13B3 variant, and they arrived by sea to Gdańsk[1] on board the ORP *Warta* transport vessel, and from there went by train to Puck. In a similar way two more airplanes arrived in Puck, this time in the H-13E version. As all the flying boats were delivered disassembled and packed in wooden crates, it was necessary to assemble them, perform technical inspection and finally to test-fly them. This work was done in March 1925 at the *MDLot.* workshop, and supervised by the Frenchman Lucien Bourdin, factory pilot of the Loiré et Oliver plant. His task was also to train all *MDLot.* pilots on this type of the aircraft. The first was pilot 2nd Lt. Adolf Stemkowski. This took place in June 1925. The aircraft were flown much and often, because it was necessary to familiarize Polish pilots with the specifics of flying on large, twin-engine flying boats, previously not used in Puck. The LeO H-13B3 and LeO H-13E were the first modern and brand new flying boats used by Polish naval aviation. They were an unquestionable qualitative leap compared to the German seaplanes dating from the last years of World War One, and also the heavily worn out and unreliable Nieuport Macchi M-9s. The LeO H-13s, however, did not gain recognition in the eyes of pilots. Pilot Cpt. Bolesław Filianowicz criticised them for the poor quality of material used for their production, poor quality of workmanship and bad protection against the destructive effects of seawater. It is worth noting that the Polish opinion was not unique. Originally, it was planned to purchase four more flying boats of this type, but eventually the order was cancelled. The LeO H-13 aircraft in

1 The unloading of military material for Poland, delivered by sea to Gdańsk, took place at the Military Transit Depot at Westerplatte.

47

[47]: The flying boat LeO H-13B3 No. 1 during pulling onto the apron of the base in Puck (Tomasz J. Kopański coll.)

48

[48]: The LeO H-13B3 flying boat is towed to the shore. As we can see the numbers were painted only on the port side. The second aircraft of this type is visible in the waters of the Bay of Puck in the left part of the photo. (City of Warsaw Archives)

49

[49]: The flying boat LeO H-13B3 No. 1-1 prepared for launching and take-off. The machine is still on the transport cart, but the crew have taken their seats already and the engines are working. Note the pilot's headgear – a square-topped cap. (City of Warsaw Archives)

[50]: Launching of the flying boat LeO H-13B3 No. 1-2. (City of Warsaw Archives)

50

[51]: The same aircraft pulled ashore after the flight. (City of Warsaw Archives)

51

[52]: *The LeO H-13B flying boat a moment after having been launched. Note, there is a part of the Puck base's slipway on the right. (Bourdin family archive via J. Fernandez)*

both variants were to become the basic type of the flying boats in the French naval aviation, but this finally did not happen.

Having been assembled and trial-flown, on 15 August 1925, the flying boats pilot Lt. Adolf Stempkowski was ordered by the *MDLot.*'s officer commanding to perform a test flight, and afterwards received permission for solo flights and flights with crews. After the new equipment had been entered onto the unit's records by the Technical and Reception Commission of *MDLot.*, a period of pilot training began. Since no such large and two-engined machines had been used at Puck so far, the training had to be carried out by an experienced pilot, familiar with the specifics of piloting such aircraft. The responsibilities of the pilot-instructor were entrusted to Lucien Bourdin, who remained in Puck until 1926. The flight programme was very intense. The idea was to make Polish pilots – at the time when the French flying boats became the basic equipment of the *MDLot.* – gain the appropriate skills and habits necessary to fly modern equipment. When as the unit's records show, the LeO H-13B3 planes were assigned to the Naval Observation Flight, while the LeO H-13Es were included in the Training Section.

A lot of interest was caused by the arrival of new flying boats in Puck, which used by the command of *MDLot.* to popularize naval aviation with the public, not only in the town itself. However, winning the favour of the Puck residents was a very important matter, because after the tragic aviation show of 1922, the relations between the sea airmen and the town residents were not the best.[2] From April 1925, a number of large-scale events were organized at the unit's facilities, during which new flying equipment was demonstrated, as well as passenger flights performed. The propaganda effect was therefore fully achieved, the relations between the inhabitants of Puck and the sea airmen significantly improved.

All four LeO H-13 flying boats remained in operational service until 1928. Later this number decreased, in 1930 there were three flying boats remaining in the records of the *MDLot*, and a year later when airplanes of this type were finally withdrawn from the line, two machines remained in service. The Leo H-13E No. 1-3 during its service also had a movie episode. In 1927 it was used in the making of "*Zew Morza*" ("Call of the Sea") directed by Henryk Szaro. Later, this aircraft was assigned to the Riverine Air Platoon in Pińsk in the Polesie marshes, as an experiment. It served with this sub-unit from 1 January 1929 and again from 16 May to 2 August 1930. The landings on the water were carried out, among others, in Pinsk and Narycz. The flying boat also took part in the celebration of the Pinsk Flotilla Day on 3 July 1930, performing demonstration flights and landing on the Lake Horodyszcze. On 1 September 1930 it was damaged in the area of Mosty Wolańskie.

Less fortunate was flying boat No. 1-4. On 29 July 1931, during a take-off from the Bay of Puck manned by a crew consisting of pilot Pettty Officer Franciszek Szatkowski and Able Seamen Bernard Gackowski and Paweł Borzyszkowski, loss of power of both engines occurred. After a brief inspection, attempts were made to take off again towards the mainland

2 During the Soldier's Day on 15 August 1922, an air show was organized – acrobatics, live fire from the air and bombing. The latter was performed manually from a Lübeck Travemünde F-2 seaplane. One of the 12.5kg bombs dropped from the hands of the observer and exploded among the spectators gathered at the Bay of Puck. Five civilians were killed, another 13 were wounded. After this accident, the unit's commanding officer pilot Cpt. Wiktoryn Kaczyński lost his post and was removed from the army, while the military official Aleksander Witkowski, who performed the unlucky bomb drop, was sentenced to arrest.

53

[53]: Let's fly, fly as much as possible! A LeO H-13B flying boat in the waters of the Bay of Puck photographed from a second machine of this type. (Bourdin family archive via J. Fernandez)

54

[54]: It is more chilly in the air! The flying boat LeO H-13B during the next flight somewhere over Kashubian region. Note the lack of the chequerboards on the top surfaces of the wings, as well as a rather nonchalant pose of the front gunner/observer. (Bourdin family archive via J. Fernandez)

[55]: Another successful flight! A LeO H-13B flying boat pulled ashore. The quality of the photo and the setting of the machine do not allow to determine the number and the marking pattern. (Bourdin family archive via J. Fernandez)

55

[56]: Refuelling the tank located in the upper wing. At a height of several meters, this was not an easy job and required the work of several men. (Bourdin family archive via J. Fernandez)

56

[57–59]: This sequence of photographs depicts the mooring of the LeO H-13E flying boat No. 1-3. (Bourdin family archive via J. Fernandez)

57

58

59

60

[60-63]: Landing to the shore of the LeO H-13E flying boat No. 1-4 after a flight had been completed. It is possible that both sequences of pictures were taken at the same time. (Bourdin family archive via J. Fernandez)

61

62

63

over the riverbed of the River Płonica. At the third attempt, when they managed to get to 80-100 metres altitude, the engines failed due to overheating. The right engine fell silent completely, so the pilot turned back to land in the waters of the Bay of Puck, but he did not manage to fly to it, it lacked enough height. The flying boat hooked a telephone cable and crashed onto a meadow about a dozen meters from the shoreline. The front of the hull broke away and flew off for several metres, also the engines broke free of the nacelles and fell on the pilots' cockpit. The crew suffered serious injuries, but fortunately the incident ended without fatalities. The cause of the accident was overheating of one of the engines and poor air-carrying capacity on that day.

At the end of 1931, one of the LeO H-13 B flying boats was also destroyed when it crashed, but there is no confirmed information on its number. Most probably, it was machine No. 1-2. The crew of the aircraft were pilots Lt. Roman Borowiec, Lt. Antoni Wacięga, observer Lt. Józef Rudzki and mechanic Petty Officer Sebastian Olbert. During the take-off, the hull hit the water and a large section of the bottom skin broke off the nose part. The observer, not wanting to fall through this gap into the water, was holding on to the machine gun's turntable. The damage to the aircraft was also seen by Petty Officer Józef Tylec, who was monitoring the take-off from a speedboat and initiated the rescue action. When attempting to land, the machine fell into the water and partially sank, the crew survived.

[64]: Taking up position in the front gunner/observer seat as well as in the pilots' cockpit of the LeO H-13E flying boat required climbing to a height of several metres with a ladder. Note the small white number 3 painted on the transport cart, which suggests that these carts were individually assigned to each flying boat. (Bourdin family archive via J. Fernandez)

64

Periods of service and assignments of the Leo H-13B3/E flying boats

Type	No.	Delivered	Assignments in *MDLot.*	Scrapped	Notes
LeO H-13B3	1-1	19.11.1924	1924–1929 – Naval Observation Flight	31.12.1929	-
LeO H-13B3	1-2	1.01.1925	1925–1931 – Naval Observation Flight	1931	Damaged during take-off
LeO H-13E	1-3	1.01.1925	1925–1928 – Training Section 1929–1930 – Riverine Air Platoon	1930	Damaged during landing at Mosty Wolańskie on 1.09.1928
LeO H-13E	1-4	1.01.1925	1925–1929 – Naval Observation Flight/Training Section 1930–1931 – Training Section	30.08.1931	Crashed during take-off on 29.08.1931

65

[65-66]: The Pińsk Riverine Flotilla Day in Horodyszcze, 1930. The flying boat LeO H-13E No. 1-3 is visible together with the ORP Admirał Sierpinek *HQ boat. (NAC Archives)*

66

[67]: The flying boat LeO H-13E No. 1-4 prepared for launching. The aircraft is placed on a transport cart, with which it will be pushed down the slipway into the water. The crew of the aircraft are already at their positions. The characteristic helmets are noteworthy. (Polish Navy Museum in Gdynia)

67

[68]: The flying boat LeO H-13B3 No. 1-1, Morska Eskadra Obserwacyjna *(Naval Observation Flight), Puck, June 1925. The airplane in factory finish. The upper part of the fuselage and fuel tank on the upper wing are painted blue-grey* (Gris Bleu Foncé)*, side surfaces of the fuselage, upper and lower surfaces of the wings and the horizontal rudder are light grey-blue* (Gris Bleu Clair)*. The engine nacelles are in a natural metal (aluminium). An early variant of the marking pattern, referring to the French naval aviation "N" the form of a black anchor is painted in the nose part and a black number N:1. The markings were painted only on the port side. The numerical designations of the aircraft were also painted on the vertical stabilizer on both sides.*

68

[69]: The LeO H-13B3 flying boat No. 1 anchored by the beach in Gdynia. The airplane is in French factory finish. On the bow, "borrowed" from the French naval aviation markings in the form of a black anchor entwined by a chain and a digit. Note also the black square painted in front of the number and the vertical safety propeller stripe, probably painted in red. (MOW in Hel)

69

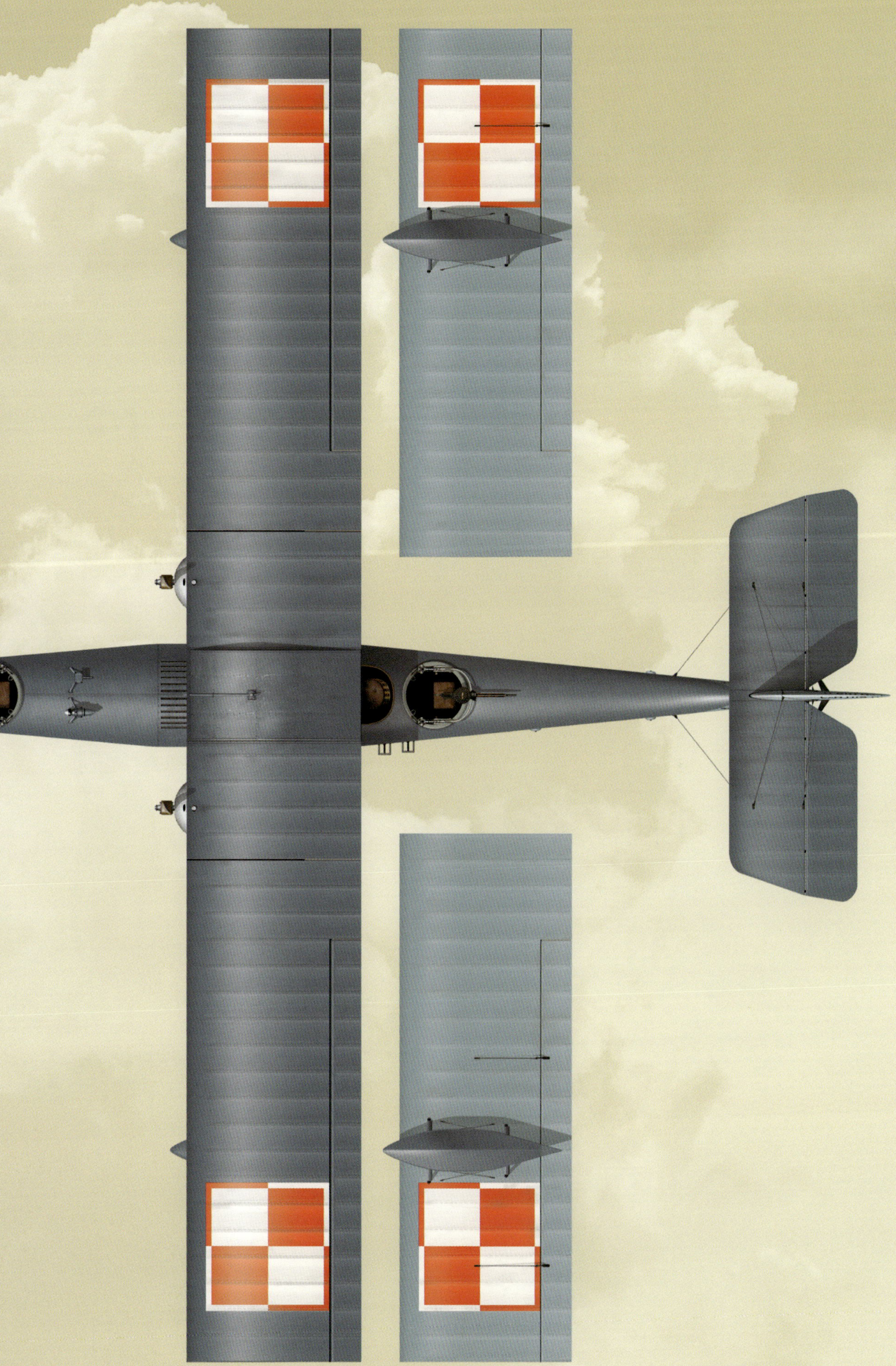

[70]: The LeO H-13B3 flying boat No. 1-1 of the Eskadra Wielosilnikowa (Multi-Engine Flight), Puck 1924. The airplane is in factory painting scheme.

70

71

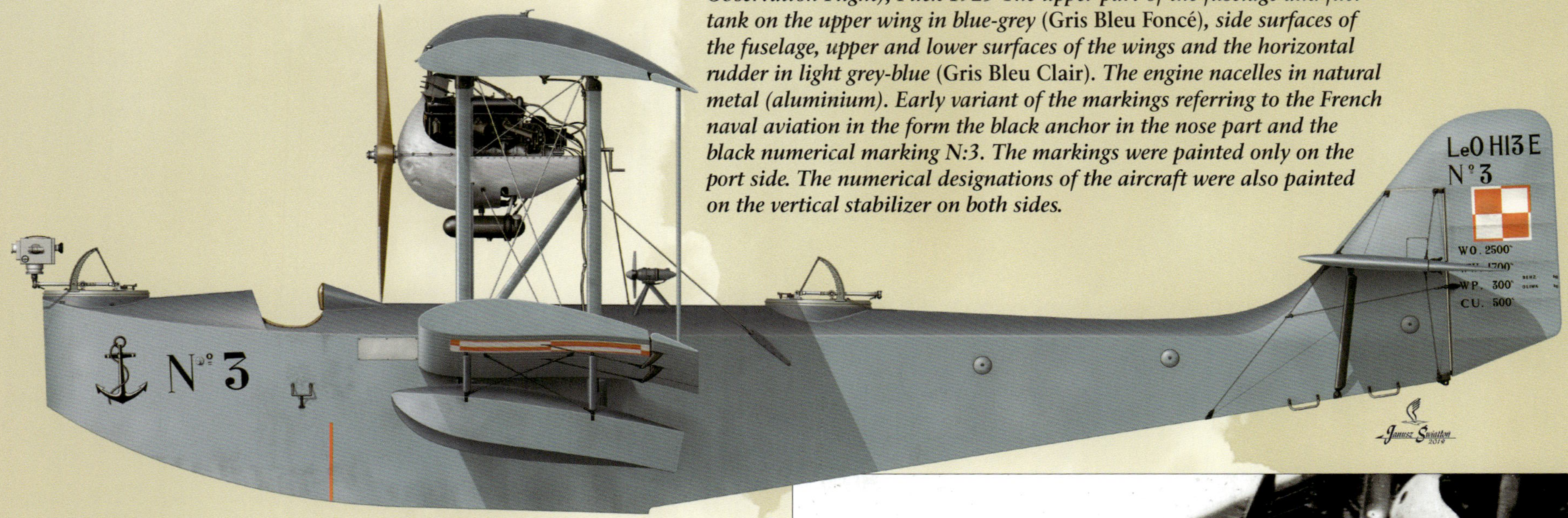

[71]: The LeO H-13E No. 1-3, the Morska Eskadra Obserwacyjna *(Naval Observation Flight), Puck 1925 The upper part of the fuselage and fuel tank on the upper wing in blue-grey* (Gris Bleu Foncé)*, side surfaces of the fuselage, upper and lower surfaces of the wings and the horizontal rudder in light grey-blue* (Gris Bleu Clair)*. The engine nacelles in natural metal (aluminium). Early variant of the markings referring to the French naval aviation in the form the black anchor in the nose part and the black numerical marking N:3. The markings were painted only on the port side. The numerical designations of the aircraft were also painted on the vertical stabilizer on both sides.*

72

73

[72-73]: Preparations for the training flight of the LeO H-13E No. 1-3. At the front gunner/observer position not only machine guns can be installed but also a camera. (Bourdin family archive via J. Fernandez)

74

[74]: The crew at their posts, one can take off. The details of the construction of the front part of the LeO H-13E No. 1-3 flying boat are clearly visible, as well as the French pattern of the aircraft markings. (Bourdin family archive via J. Fernandez)

75

[75]: LeO H-13E No. 1-4, the Sekcja Ćwiczeń *(Training Section), Puck 1927. The camouflage and markings scheme is the one introduced around 1927. All top and side surfaces painted in grey-blue* (Gris Bleu Foncé), *lower surfaces in light grey-blue* (Gris Bleu Clair). *The engine nacelles in natural metal (aluminium). A large chequerboard with an inverted square layout is painted in the nose section on both sides, a white number reduced to a single digit 4 in the middle part of the fuselage.*

76

[75]: LeO H-13E flying boat set on a transport cart and trestles. The airplane is in the camouflage scheme introduced in 1927. (Wojtek Matusiak coll.)

[77]: LeO H-13E No. 1-3, the Sekcja Ćwiczeń *(Exercise Section), Puck 1927 The camouflage and markings scheme introduced around 1927. All top and side surfaces painted in grey-blue* (Gris Bleu Foncé), *lower surfaces in light grey-blue* (Gris Bleu Clair). *The engine nacelles in a natural metal (aluminium). Large chequerboard painted in the nose part on both sides, white number 1-3 in the middle of the fuselage. Both fuselage chequerboards with an inverted square layout.*

77

78

[78]: The LeO H-13E flying boat No. 1-3 on the apron of the MDLot. *base in Puck. In the background, the so-called "Pilot house" can be seen. The airplane sports the painting scheme introduced around 1927. Its characteristic feature was a large chequerboard painted in the nose part of the aircraft and a white number in the middle part of the fuselage. (Wiesław Bączkowski archives from Stratus coll.)*

[79]: LeO H-13E No. 1-3, the Sekcja Ćwiczeń *(Training Section), Puck 1927. The camouflage and markings pattern introduced around 1927.*

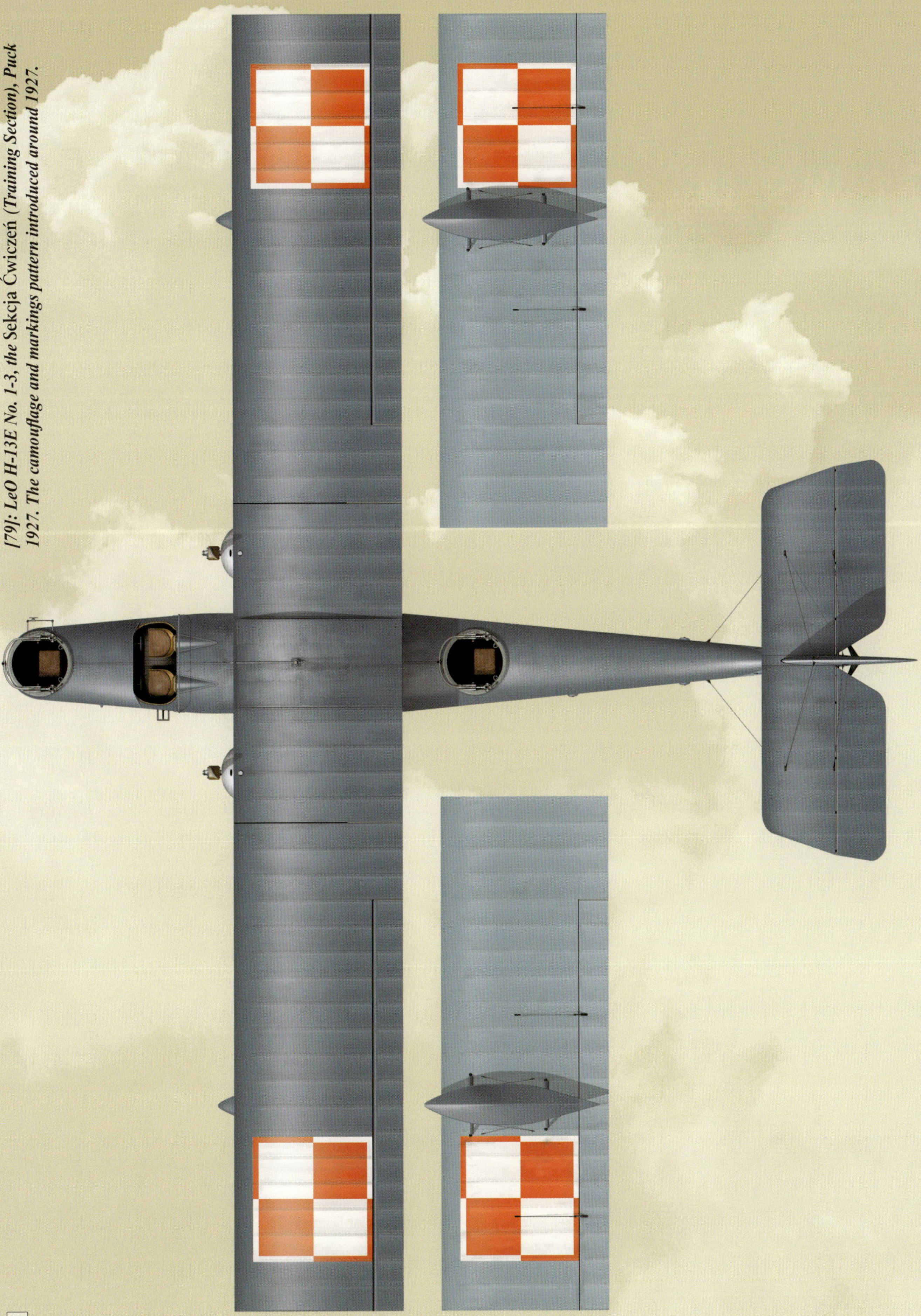

79

CAMS 30E

For training purposes, four flying boats of the CAMS 30E type were delivered to Puck. This was a relatively new design, developed in 1923–1924 at the *Chantiers Aéro-Maritimes de la Seine* (CAMS) plant in Paris. The design was developed under the supervision of Ing. Raffaele Conflenti. It was a single-engine flying boat with a wooden structure and biplane arrangement. It had a flat bottom fuselage with step and an open crew cabin. Pilot/instructor occupied the right-hand side, the student/observer on the left. The controls were duplicated. The fuselage skin was made of plywood. Both wings had a wooden two-spar structure covered with canvas, the upper plane was supported on struts made of duralumin tubes and braced with steel stringers. Ailerons were placed on the upper plane. The vertical rudder was covered with plywood, and all control surfaces were covered with canvas. Horizontal tailplanes were supported by struts to the hull. The flying boat also had stabilizing floats placed under the lower wing. Power came from an eight-cylinder Hispano Suiza 8E engine with an output of 150 hp supported on struts between the upper wing and fuselage.

Because the CAMS 30E did not enter service with France's naval aviation, it was produced in a small series which were designated from A to E depending on the country to which they were exported. The main task of these seaplanes was training, but they could also be used to perform reconnaissance missions. Four flying boats of this type purchased by Poland were delivered in 1925, and they arrived in Puck a year later. Then they were assembled and test flown by pilot 2nd Lt. Adolf Stempkowski. The new training flying boats replaced the scrapped Nieuport Macchi M-9s. They were incorporated into the Training Section and then to the Training Flight. Sometimes, they also served with the Naval Observation Flight.

The CAMS 30E flying boats did not enjoy a good opinion among the *MDLot.* personnel. They were quite dangerous to fly, and the long straight hull had a tendency to break at take-off and landing even on a small wave. It was a training seaplane, but only for those who already had some experience in piloting flying boats. Nevertheless, no fatal accident occurred on them, and CAMS 30Es flew frequently.

The CAMS 30Es' flying service lasted until 1930. On 10 April 1930, the *MDLot.'s* commanding officer ordered all flying boats of this type to be assigned for scrap. A little later, on 11 May 1930, a crash occurred on the Bay of Puck, as a result of which CAMS 30E No. 2-4 was damaged. Later, its fuselage was used as a caravan after the wings had been disassembled. In 1931, the last operational flying boat of this type was damaged (No. 2-2). A year later, it was used as an exhibit at a display organized as part of the 8th Propaganda Week of the *L.O.P.P.* ("Anti-Aircraft and Anti-Gas Defence League"), which took place on 7–12 July 1931.

In 1932, two fuselages of two CAMS 30E aircraft withdrawn from service were used to construct a planing vessel on the catamaran system, employed to learn how to take off and land in conditions close to reality. Both fuselages were joined with a section of wing. The drive was a 180 HP engine powering a four-blade propeller. The machine was designed by pilot 2nd Lt. Gustaw Sidorowicz, he also supervised its construction, performed by the students of the Seaplane Maintenance Course.

[80]: A group of naval airmen poses for a photo next to a CAMS 30E training flying boat. The chequerboards painted on the horizontal tailplane can be clearly seen. The photo does not allow identification of the number the machine sports. The aircraft had all chequerboards with reverse order of squares. (MOW in Hel)

80

Periods of service and assignments of the CAMS 30E flying boats:

Type	Number	Delivered	*MDLot.* assignments	Withdrawn	Notes
CAMS 30E	2-1	1926	1926-1929 – Training Section/Naval Observation Flight	10.04.1930	-
CAMS 30E	2-2	1926	1926-1929 – Training Section/Naval Observation Flight	30.04.1930	-
CAMS 30E	2-3	1926	1926-1929 – Training Section/Naval Observation Flight	30.11.1929	-
CAMS 30E	2-4	1926	1926-1929 – Training Section/Naval Observation Flight	30.11.1929	After having been withdrawn displayed during the 8th Week of the *L.O.P.P.* 5-12.08.1931. Fuselage later used as a caravan.

81

[81]: The CAMS 30E flying boat No. 2-3 in front of one of the hangars at the base in Puck. The aircraft has an early type of markings, and there is a dash between the two digits. Inscriptions on the vertical rudder are white. The chequer-boards have an inverted square layout. The photo was taken on 9 April 1927. In the cockpit, observer Lt. Tadeusz Gondek. (Tomasz J. Kopański coll.)

82

[82]: A commemorative photo of the CAMS 30E flying boat No. 23 taken at the base of the Naval Air Squadron in Puck. In the background, a crane for servicing flying boats is visible. (MOW in Hel).

[83]: The CAMS 30E No. 23, the Sekcja Ćwiczeń *(Training Section), Puck 1929. The airplane is in factory finish. Blue-grey (*Gris Bleu Foncé*) on all upper and side surfaces, and engine nacelles, lower surfaces of wings and horizontal tail planes in light grey (*Gris Clair*). Fuselage to the waterline painted in black (*noir*). A variant of marking in the form of a white, two-digit number not separated by a dash, painted on the nose on both sides. On the vertical stabilizer there are numerical and weight markings in white.*

83

84

[84]: The CAMS 30E flying boat No. 23 photographed at the base of the Naval Air Squadron in Puck. Numerical variant with no dash in between digits. Inscriptions on the vertical stabilizer in white. The chequerboards have reverse order of squares. (MOW in Hel)

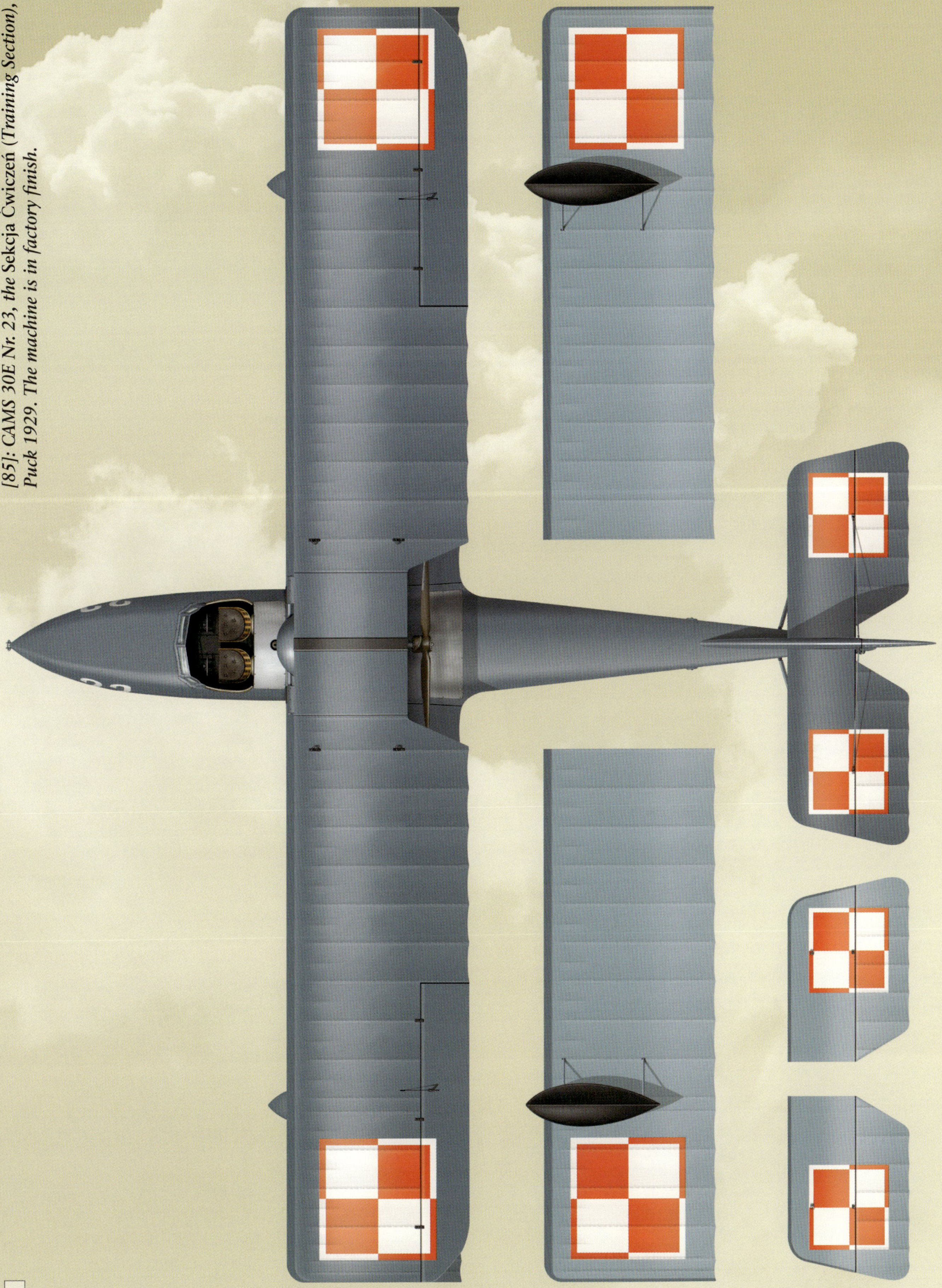

[85]: CAMS 30E Nr. 23, the Sekcja Ćwiczeń (Training Section), Puck 1929. The machine is in factory finish.

85

86

[86]: CAMS 30E No. 2-4, the Sekcja Ćwiczeń *(Training Section), Puck 1927, in factory finish. Blue-grey (*Gris Bleu Foncé*) on all upper and side surfaces as well as engine nacelles, bottom surfaces of wings and horizontal tail planes in light grey (*Gris Clair*). Fuselage below the waterline in black (*noir*). Marking variant in the form of a two-digit white number painted in the nose on both sides, digits separated by a dash. The trademark of the CAMS label is painted in front of the number. The numerical and weight markings painted in white on the vertical stabilizer.*

87

[87]: The CAMS 30E flying boat 2-4 during landing by the beach in Gdynia. Markings according to the early pattern, digits separated by a dash. (Tomasz J. Kopański coll.)

88

*[88]: CAMS 30E No. 2-2, Puck, July 1931. The aircraft after it had been withdrawn from service, in factory finish. The Blue-grey (*Gris Bleu Foncé*) on all upper and side surfaces and engine nacelles, lower surfaces of the wings and horizontal tail planes in light grey (*Gris Clair*). Fuselage to the waterline in black (*noir*). Temporary inscription reads as follows* "VIII tydzień L.O.P.P. 5/VII – 12/VII" *("8th Week of the L.O.P.P. 5/VII – 12/VII").*

89

[89]: The CAMS 30E flying boat No. 2-2 sporting a temporary scheme for the 8th Propaganda Week of the L.O.P.P., 5–12 July 1931. An inscription was placed on the fuselage – "VIII tydzień L.O.P.P. 5/VII – 12/VII" – probably painted in white. The airplane sports the standard French camouflage pattern. The photo does not allow determination of what number the machine was marked with. The photo was taken at the MDLot. base in Puck after the withdrawal of the CAMS 30E flying boats from active service. (MOW in Hel)

Latham 43 HB.3

Having abandoned the idea of purchasing more LeO H-13B3 flying boats, *Wojskowy Zakład Zaopatrzenia Aeronautyki (WZZA)* – the Military Aeronautics Supply Department – chose another airplane, which in time became the symbol and showcase of the *MDLot.* in its best years. We are speaking of the Latham 43 HB.3 heavy flying boat. It was also a reconnaissance and assault machine, similar construction-wise to the LeO H-13B3. However, it was much better designed and had much better performance. The fuselage had a boat structure with a profiled bottom together with the step, which enabled safe take-off and landing even at high speeds. The bow waves spread flat to the sides and reconnected to each other behind the tail of the aircraft, creating a characteristic wake, which in no way interfered with the machine moving on the water. The crew consisted of four men with three open cockpits at their disposal. In the nose of the machine there was a gunner/radio operator's post, it was equipped with a turntable mounting two machine guns. A communication shaft running inside the hull, along the axis of symmetry, connected this cockpit with another one, located just in front of the wing chamber. It was occupied by the pilot, sitting on the left side with an observer to his right. The cabin was protected by a windscreen. The communication shaft connected it with the third cabin, located behind the wing chamber. There was a tail gunner/radio operator's post. This cabin was also equipped with a machine gun turntable. There was also a wireless set, powered by electricity from a generator driven by the wind during flight. The fuselage had a plywood skin. The aircraft was of biplane structure with double-spar planes covered with canvas. The lower plane was equipped with stabilizing floats, while the upper one was supported on struts made of duralumin tubes braced with steel cable tie-rods. The tail was also covered with canvas. The horizontal tailplane was additionally supported, as with the lower wing, to the fuselage by means of struts. Power came from two Lorraine-Dietrich L 4 V-8 engines placed side-by-side, each with 400 HP output. Both engines were eight-cylinder power units on the V system. Both engines were placed on trestles made of steel tubes, which were placed on the central part of the wing chamber. The engines were started manually by means of a crank. The engines were liquid cooled, radiators were placed on the side of each engine on the inner posts of the trestle. The fuel tank was located in the middle part of the

90

[90]: The NCO Course, Aircraft Maintenance Platoon, class of 1929, the men pose against the background of the Latham 43 HB.3 flying boat No. 3-1. It is worth paying attention to the models of flying boats displayed on the propeller and in front of it. These models have survived to date and are exhibits at the Muzeum Ziemi Puckiej – *Museum of the Puck Land. (Mariusz Konarski coll.)*

[91]: Parade of the MDLot. *sub-units on the unit's day, 15 July 1927. Of course, the exhibition of flying equipment could not be missed on such the occasion. In front of the hangar, two Latham 43 HB.3 Nos. 3-1 and 3-2 and LeO H-13E flying boats were displayed. (Muzeum Ziemi Puckiej)*

91

upper plane. The engines powered two two-blade propellers manufactured by the Szomański company. These aircraft also had very powerful weaponry. Bomb racks, placed under the bottom plane on both sides of the fuselage allowed for carrying a load of a total weight from 400 to 600 kg, and on each turntable it was possible to install two machine guns, which were 7.69 mm calibre Lewis or 7.7 mm Vickers.

The order to buy machines of this type was received by the Polish Military Acquisitions Mission in Paris at the end of June 1924. Eight aircraft were bought, one of which was ordered with dual controls, intended for pilot training, and one was adapted for towing targets. The airplanes were delivered to Poland by sea to the Military Transit Depot at Westerplatte, and then they were delivered by rail to Puck. After assembling and test flying, they were put onto the unit's equipment listing. Six machines served initially in the 2nd Naval Assault Flight, which at the turn of 1928–1929 was renamed the Multi-Engine Naval Flight. In 1930 the unit once again changed its name to the 1st Line Flight "Wiking". Two airplanes were always kept in reserve, sporadically single aircraft were assigned to the Naval Observation Flight.

They were the largest flying boats that served with the *MDLot.* throughout its entire existence. Their size and performance were second only to the CANT Z.506B Airone bomber and torpedo aircraft. The main advantage of the Latham was its huge range, allowing it to stay in the air for up to seven hours which made it possible to perform long patrol flights outside Polish territorial waters and the observation of flights of foreign aircraft and movements of foreign ships. The enormous Lathams very quickly gained the liking of the crews. They were very stable in flight. In good weather conditions, the airplane was so balanced that it was possible to take the hands off the controls and maintain course only with the help of the rudder bar. Problems only began when the weather changed, then the size and weight of the aircraft became apparent. Impressions of flying these machines were gathered by Andrzej Celarek:

"It was difficult for beginners to endure in the Latham, two two-metre propellers were working half a metre behind the pilots' cabin, and when they got out, something still roared in their heads for the two next days. The pilots from Puck then noticed that the secret was to fly a lot. When they flew every day, the noise in their heads somehow disappeared and only a long flight after the first break was again hard (...)

Pilot Petty Officer Henryk Wiechciński had his own approach to the Latham. When he sensed that the aircraft was about to rise up in some invisible air column – he trampled the rudder bar several times. Such a swaying with the great steering rudder acted like an aerodynamic brake, and the machine lost some speed, the planes lost some lift, and the heavy winged boat went through the climb area sedately, without making an unexpected rise – and that usually meant trouble. The crews involved in the fleet exercises attempted to establish radio communication with surface ships.

92

[92–93]: A tracked tractor was used to roll the Latham 43 HB.3 heavy flying boats around the base. In the picture, a group of MDLot. *officers and other ranks pose at the Latham 43 HB.3 No. 3-1 flying boat together with this tractor. Fourth from the left in a leather jacket is pilot – Cpt. Bolesław Filanowicz. (Tomasz J. Kopański coll.)*

93

94

[94]: The so-called "Little Beach" in Hel was popular among holiday-makers due to the inshore shallows and always warm water. This time an additional attraction was two Latham 43 HB.3 flying boats anchored near the shoreline. In the foreground, the machine sporting No. 3-4. In the background on the left the Evangelical Church in Hel can be seen and the facilities of the fishing harbour. (Mariusz Konarski coll.)

95

[95]: Latham 43 HB.3 from the 1st Line Flight "Wiking" this time was the attraction of the beach in Jurata. The plane has all chequerboards painted with an inverted square layout. Three dark (red?) stripes are noteworthy, painted in the rear part of the fuselage. (Wincenty Kobylański coll. via Wiktor Kobylański)

96

[96]: Another photograph of the same machine. Note the Training Flight insignia painted at the bow. (Wincenty Kobylański coll. via Wiktor Kobylański)

They "attempted" – for the weak contemporary wireless sets on the flying boats were not heard very much on the ships, and in the rumbling box of the Latham, only the roar of engines and nothing more was heard. During a flight the crew communicated in sign language or by means of written messages"[1].

However, one man found a way to effectively communicate with ships using the radio. Andrzej Celarek again:

"The headquarters after each exercise ascertained with amazement that the only radio mechanic, who was getting in touch with the fleet was Petty Officer Wzorek. This later long-time lighthouse keeper at Rozewie, for a time guarded the secret of his successes, but eventually he disclosed it.

Before each transmission, he signalled to the pilot: Full blast! The pilot also steered the machine into a shallow diving flight, the speed temporarily increased to the acceptable limit – which was indeed a modest 180 km/hour, but the fan driven generator gave a slightly higher voltage and signals from the aircraft somehow reached the receivers on the ships. When switching to reception, the pilot reduced the speed to a minimum, the hellish pounding slightly decreased and Wzorek had a better chance of hearing something in his headphones"[2].

1 Andrzej Celarek, Morski Dywizjon Lotniczy. Wspomnienia pilotów, DJ, Gdańsk 2002, p. 60, 63.

2 Idem, pp. 63–64

It is no wonder that having flying boats with such good properties in the unit, these machines were flown much and often. Although they were mainly assigned to the line flights, initially to the Naval Multi-Engine Flight and later to the 1st Line Flight "Wiking", the aircraft were often used for training as well. Newcomers to the *MDLot.* were trained on them as well.

However, the flights were not limited only to the off-coast area and the southern Baltic. A series of flights to various destinations around the country were performed and the flying boats landed on rivers or lakes.

Long distance flights performed in Poland by the Latham 43 HB.3 flying boats

Departure date	Aircraft No.	Route
13.07.1928	3-2	Puck – Toruń – Puck
14.05.1929	3-3	Puck – Warszawa – Dęblin – Puck
27.05.1929	3-1	Puck – Toruń – Puck
11.06.1929	3-6	Puck – Toruń – Bydgoszcz – Puck
11.08.1929	3-6	Puck – Warszawa – Dęblin – Puck
22.07.1929	3-1	Puck – Warszawa – Grudziądz – Puck
1.09.1929	3-4	Puck – Tczew – Puck
11.05.1930	3-4	Puck – Tyniec – Puck
16.05.1930	3-1	Puck – Warszawa – Dęblin – Puck
11.10.1930	3-8	Puck – Warszawa – Puck

97

[97]: A slightly different image depicting the same scene. The construction in the foreground is one of the three concrete pedestals of the harbour crane. In this photo you can also see that the Latham 43 HB.3 No. 7 of the Training Flight had properly painted chequerboards also on the vertical stabilizer. (MOW in Hel)

[98]: The Latham 43 HB.3 heavy flying boat No. 7 of the Training Flight being towed to the shore. The airplane is probably damaged, as evidenced by the strangely submerged fuselage. On the bow, there is the insignia of the Training Flight, the chequerboards on the lower surfaces of the wings and the horizontal tail planes are painted correctly. (MOW in Hel)

98

99

[99]: Sometimes a take-off had to be performed in choppy waters. Here we see Latham 43 HB.3 flying boat No. 3-2. This aircraft had chequerboards on the vertical stabilizer painted in the proper way. On the top surfaces of the wings and the horizontal tail planes, the correct arrangement of squares was not applied though. (MOW in Hel)

The period of intensive use of the Latham 43 HB.3 flying boats in the Naval Air Squadron also coincided with a number of visits that pilots from other countries paid to the Puck unit. Among others, there were pilots from Denmark, Italy and Britain. It was inevitable that the Poles made return visits in these countries, the representatives of which had been previously hosted in Puck. Because Latham 43 HB.3 flying boats were the most suitable for performing long-distance flights, they were used for foreign visits.

The first foreign visit took place on 17–21 August 1928. Aircraft Nos. 3-3 (crew: 2nd Lt. Cmdr. Karol Trzasko-Durski, Lt. Eugeniusz Podolski, Lt. Edward Suzanowicz, Junior Craftsman Stanisław Potrawiak, 2nd Craftsman Czesław Sliwoniuk) and 3-4 (crew: Cpt. Bolesław Filanowicz, Cpt. Edward Szystowski, Lt Adolf Stempkowski, Jun. Craftsman Marcin Strenek, 2nd Craftstman Michał Połoszynowicz) visited Copenhagen. The start took place at 0755 hrs and the flight itself was performed in favourable weather conditions. Arrival at Copenhagen was as planned. The stay in Denmark lasted three days, Polish pilots visited the Polish Embassy in Denmark, as well as Danish naval airmen. The airplanes returned to Puck separately, the first on 20 August 1928 when the crew of the No. 3-3 machine arrived, while on the next day aircraft No. 3-4 landed. It was the first foreign visit of the Puck pilots and it could be regarded as a success for the unit.

The next foreign flight took place two weeks later. This time the destination of the visit was the Latvian capital Riga. The same machines were selected for the flight, but their crews changed slightly. On No. 3-3 the crew was composed of 2nd Lt. Cmdr. Karol Trzasko – Durski, Lt. Eugeniusz Podolski, Petty Officer Henryk Wiechciński, 2nd Craftsman Władysław Łabudzki, Cpl.Władysław Szopa. On machine No. 3-4 flew Lt. Adolf Stempkowski, Petty Officer Franciszek Wardliński, Lt. Kazimierz Żuchowicz, Chief Craftsman Marcin Strnek and

100

[100]: To get on or off such an enormous airplane as the Latham 43 HB.3 it was necessary to use a ladder. In the picture, machine No. 3-4 is being lifted from the water. (Mariusz Konarski coll.)

[101]: *A group of naval airmen with the Latham 43 HB.3 flying boat No. 3-3. The airplane is placed on a wooden transport cart. On the bottom surfaces of the lower wing the bomb rack assembly can be seen. At the fore gunner's post, there is also an electric generator supplying the wireless set. The picture was taken on 6 April 1928 before the departure of three Latham 43 HB.3s on an official visit to Riga. (Mariusz Konarski coll.)*

[102]: *A huge Latham 43 HB.3 dwarfing the tiny Morane Saulnier MS-35 AR/EP trainer like David and Goliath in a photograph taken in Puck. (Muzeum Ziemi Puckiej)*

Junior Craftsman Stanisław Potrawiak. The start took place on 6 September 1928 at 0640 hrs. Also this time the flight took place in good atmospheric conditions at an altitude of 700 metres and lasted 4 hours and 45 minutes. In Riga, the Polish pilots stayed three days and on 9 September 1928, both machines returned to Puck without any problems. An interesting fact is that two crew members, Chief Petty Officer Henryk Wiechcinski and Petty Officer Franciszek Wardliński did not return to Puck until 11 September 1928, when they arrived by rail – on the way back, dropping by at Tallinn in Estonia. What the reason was is not known.

Both of these flights proved not only the suitability of the Latham 43 HB.3 flying boats for this type of tasks, but also had a beneficial effect on improving the morale of the unit, who had fought so long against the "land forces spirit", suffered from the times of Col. Antoni Leonkow. These operations had made the personnel of the *MDLot.* aware that they were a fully naval unit and that their area of operations was the sea.

The third foreign visit in the history of the *MDLot.* took place two years after the events described above. This time the goal of Puck's airmen was Latvian Liepaja. Also this time the flight was to be performed on Latham 43 HB.3 flying boats. Three machines were chosen for the flight:

No. 3-3, crew: 2nd Lt. Cmdr. Karol Trzasko – Durski, Petty Officer Józef Gawlik, Chief Craftsman Marcin Sternk, Craftsman Radiotechnician Władysław Wzorek;

No. 3-7, crew: Cpt. Bolesław Fialnowicz, 2nd Lt. Stefan Kryński, 2nd Lt. Walerian Jesionowski, Craftsman Stanisław Potrawiak, Craftsman Stanisław Jakubowski;

No. 3-8, crew: Lt. Bronisław Lubińkowski, 2nd Lt. Bolesław Piątkowski, 2nd Lt. Henryk Kołodziejczyk, Craftsman Konstanty Nowicki, Craftsman Bronisław Karczewski.

The take-off from Puck took place on 27 September 1930 in the morning. The 260 km long route over the high seas went without any hindrance, and after a three-day stay in Latvia, on 30 September 1930 they returned to Puck.

With reference to the long-distance flights which have been discussed above, we should mention one quite dangerous event that took place slightly earlier, on 29 June 1926. The HQ of the *MDLot.* ordered four Latham 43 HB.3 flying boats from Puck to perform a routine meteorological flight. They took off in two pairs. In the second pair there was flying boat No. 3-5, its pilot was Chief Petty Officer Henryk Wiechcinski and the observer was Obs. 2nd Lt. Henryk Kołodziejczyk. Over the sea, the flying boats fell into an area of dense fog bank. The crews lost eye contact between each other, and with time the visibility dropped to nil – the pilot could not even see the bow of the machine. It did not help to climb to a ceiling of a thousand, then two thousand, and finally three and a half thousand metres, there was still no visibility. In the end, the commander decided to reduce height to an altitude at which something can be seen. The surface of the sea was visible at

103

[103]: *The Latham 43 HB.3 flying boat No. 3-2 anchored by the beach in Oksywie. In the background, warships are moored at the pier – type FM minesweepers and ORP "Komendant Piłsudski" and ORP "Generał Haller" gunboats. (MOW in Hel)*

[104]: *Joint manoeuvres with the fleet. The Latham 43 HB.3 flying boat No. 3-2 in the air, under its fuselage something that resembles international signal code flags is visible. Actually, it is a target panel for firing practice. Clearly visible are the chequerboards on the lower surfaces of the planes painted in the correct way. (NAC Archives)*

[105]: *Sea bathing in the shallow waters of the Bay of Puck. In the background a Latham 43 HB.3 flying boat from the 1st Line Flight "Wiking". (Grzegorz Śliżewski coll.)*

104

105

150 metres, but the fog height was lowering as well. A further reduction in height was necessary. At 10 metres Latham landed, further flight was dangerous as it was easy to hit some vessel. Landing took place around 8.30 am, after a little over one hour of flight. Around noon, the fog began to thin down. One aircraft appeared, but it was too high to see the damaged flying boat, despite the fact that the crew fired the entire supply of signal lights. The take-off attempts were also unsuccessful, the waves were too high, the engines could not reach their maximum output, and the flying boat began to take on water. About three o'clock in the afternoon, part of the canvas skin was torn off by the crew so as to reduce the pressure of the waves. On the tensioning cables between the wings some kind of sail hastily made of signal code flags was raised, the flying boat began to move a little faster, which gave hope for rescue. At about five o'clock, a warship was seen on the horizon, it was one of the Polish torpedo ships returning from Denmark. This group of ships were returning to Poland when they were ordered to search the estimated area where the aircraft had been declared missing. The torpedo ship which made contact with the damaged seaplane was the ORP "Kujawiak" commanded by 2nd Lieutenant-Commander Józef Boreyka. Almost imme-

106

[106]: September 1927, Air Week in Kraków. The MDLot. *was proudly represented, a Latham 43 HB.3 flying boat flew in from Puck, and its crew included the commanding officer of the* MDLot. *Cmdr. Karol Trzasko – Durski (in the middle with a bouquet of flowers), on the left there are Cpt. Edward Szystkowski and Lt. Eugeniusz Podolski. (NAC Archives)*

[107]: Latham 43 HB.3 flying boats during their line service performed many long-distance domestic flights. In the picture, machine No. 3-1 is moored on the Vistula river near Kraków, where it also aroused considerable interest, as evidenced by the crowd gathered on the shore. (NAC Archives)

107

108

[108]: Another attraction for vacationers. To get to the floating Latham 43 HB.3, the two officers must use a boat. (Muzeum Ziemi Puckiej)

109

[109]: We are coming back from Riga. The courtesy visit of the MDLot. *airmen to Latvia took place on 6-9 September 1928. The machines numbered 3-3 and 3-5 3-8 took part in it. On the way back the aircraft also visited Liepaja, as evidenced by the caption in the picture. (Muzeum Ziemi Puckiej)*

diately after attaching a towrope, the torpedo ship moved at a minimal speed towards Gdynia. In the end a speed of ten knots was considered safe. Only the pilot was left aboard the flying boat, but even he had to obey the clear commands of the torpedo boat skipper, and moved with the ship. Twilight fell, the Latham's fuselage was leaking more and more. If the flying boat sank in the dark, the pilot would not have had the slightest chance to survive. They arrived in Gdynia around one o'clock at night. The pilot was in Puck on the next day, and a day later he was in the air again. The Latham had to undergo some repair work, and earlier, in Gdynia, the cause of lack of sufficient engine power was discovered, when the machine tried to take off on the high seas. The heavy waves that hit the flying boat during its landing bent the short struts between the fuselage and the lower wing. This limited the possibility of moving the slider of the engine control cables, which ran there. The fault was easy to fix, but it could not be detected by the crewmen themselves on the high seas. The flying boat became operational again ten days after the unlucky landing. The Latham's crew spent approximately 18 hours at sea.

The service of these giant flying boats with the Naval Air Squadron in Puck should be considered successful and lucky. None of them ever crashed. However, there were two fatal accidents. On 21 July 1930, during a training flight, after a landing while changing seats in the cockpit, 2nd Lt. Zygmunt Podgórski was hit by a spinning propeller and killed on the spot. On 11 August 1931, Latham 43 HB.3 flying boat No. 3-1 was damaged during landing. The cause of the accident was the pilot's error, the flying boat approaching the landing suddenly lost altitude and dropped down from a height of several metres. As a result of the strong impact on the surface of the water, the hull suffered cracks and the machine began to sink. Petty Officer Józef Gawlik banged his head against the instrument panel and died instantly. It was the last fatal accident involving a French-made aircraft.

The Latham 43 HB.3 flying boats saw very active service, hence they were starting to show more and more wear and tear. Like most French production planes in the early 1930s, they were gradually phased out of service. Aircraft Nos. 3-5, 3-7 and 3-8 were withdrawn only at the turn of 1938 and 1939. They were stored at the *MDLot.* depot until the very outbreak of the war. With the withdrawal of the Lathams from active service, the *MDLot.* lost its offensive capabilities for good. They were the only true assault flying boats. Their tasks were taken over by the Lublin R-VIIIter/hydro as well as R-XIIIter/hydro and G/hydro floatplanes, but for obvious reasons they were unable to perform them. In the future the Latham 43 HB.3 operational tasks were to be taken over by the Lublin R.XX and CANT Z.506B Airone torpedo-bombers. The program to build the prototype of the former ended in failure, while entry into service by the Italian machines never materialized due to the outbreak of war.

110

[110]: A Latham 43 HB.3 heavy flying boat anchored on the Bay of Puck. A photograph from the initial period of service of these aircraft, as evidenced by the lack of a number on the nose. In the background, the Hel Peninsula is visible. (MOW in Hel)

Periods of service and assignments of the Latham 43 HB.3 flying boats

Type	No.	Delivered	Assignments within the *MDLot.*	Phased out	Notes
Latham 43 HB.3	3-1	1926	1926–1928 – Naval Assault Flight 1928–1929 – Naval Multi-Engine Flight 1930–1931 – 1st Line Flight "Wiking"	11.08.1931	Damaged when landing on the Bay of Puck. Pilot, Petty Officer Józef Gawlik killed.
Latham 43 HB.3	3-2	1926	1926–1928 – Naval Assault Flight 1928–1929 – Naval Multi-Engine Flight 1930 – 1st Line Flight "Wiking"	17.09.1930	–
Latham 43 HB.3	3-3	1926	1926–1928 – Naval Assault Flight 1928–1929 – Naval Multi-Engine Flight	30.11.1929	–
Latham 43 HB.3	3-4	1926	1926–1928 – Naval Assault Flight 1928–1929 – Naval Multi-Engine Flight	30.11.1929	–
Latham 43 HB.3	3-5	1926	1926–1928 – Naval Assault Flight 1928–1929 – Naval Multi-Engine Flight 1929 – Training Section	1929	Stored at *MDLot.* depot until 1938/1939
Latham 43 HB.3	3-6	1926	1926–1928 – Naval Assault Flight, 1928–1929 – Naval Multi-Engine Flight 1930–1931 – 1st Line Flight "Wiking"	10.08.1931	deficient
Latham 43 HB.3	3-7	1926	1926–1928 – Naval Assault Flight 1928–1929 – Naval Multi-Engine Flight 1930 – 1st Line Flight "Wiking"/Training Section	13.07.1930	Left wing damaged due to an accident, Stored at *MDLot.* depot until 1938/1939
Latham 43 HB.3	3-8	1926	1926–1928 – Naval Assault Flight 1928–1929 – Naval Multi-Engine Flight 1930–1933 – 1st Line Flight "Wiking"	Late 1933	Stored at *MDLot.* depot until 1938/1939 Airframe disassembled in 03.1939

111

[111]: The introduction of new French production aircraft to the service required implementation of many changes to the infrastructure of the base. Among others, a harbour crane was built at the jetty by means of which the heavy Latham 43 HB.3 flying boats were set onto the water or lifted from it. In the photograph machine No. 3-1 is underslung from the crane. In the foreground, the FBA 17 HE.2 flying boat No. 4-2 at a slipway (a wooden ramp inclining towards the water) prepared for putting it onto the water. In the background on the left, partly hidden by a flying boat is the building called the "House of Pilots" can be seen. (NAC Archives)

112

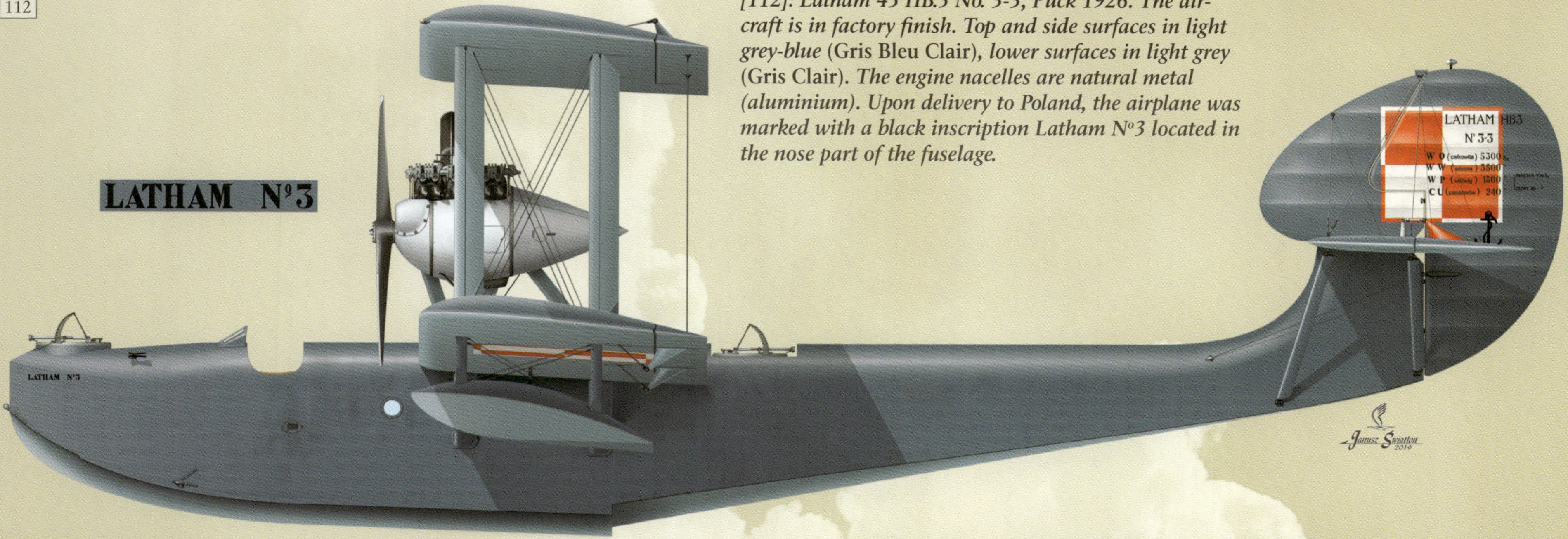

[112]: Latham 43 HB.3 No. 3-3, Puck 1926. The aircraft is in factory finish. Top and side surfaces in light grey-blue (Gris Bleu Clair), *lower surfaces in light grey* (Gris Clair). *The engine nacelles are natural metal (aluminium). Upon delivery to Poland, the airplane was marked with a black inscription Latham N°3 located in the nose part of the fuselage.*

[113]: Commemorative photograph of a group of naval airmen against the Latham 43 HB.3 heavy flying boat No. 3-3. The airplane has the chequerboards painted with the correct arrangement of squares both on the wings and on the tail section. On the bow there is a small, dark inscription, Latham No 3. It is not obvious whether its first letters have been painted over or are not visible due to the lighting. Eleventh from the left, the commanding officer of the MDLot.*, Col. Antoni Leonkow, stands centrally under the bow. (MOW in Hel)*

113

[114]: A Latham 43 HB.3 heavy flying boat on the crane at the base of the Naval Air Squadron in Puck. The lack of any markings on the fuselage is noteworthy. On the vertical stabilizer, there are chequerboards with an inverted arrangement of squares as well as an anchor and black markings "borrowed" from the French naval aviation. (MOW collections in Hel)

114

115

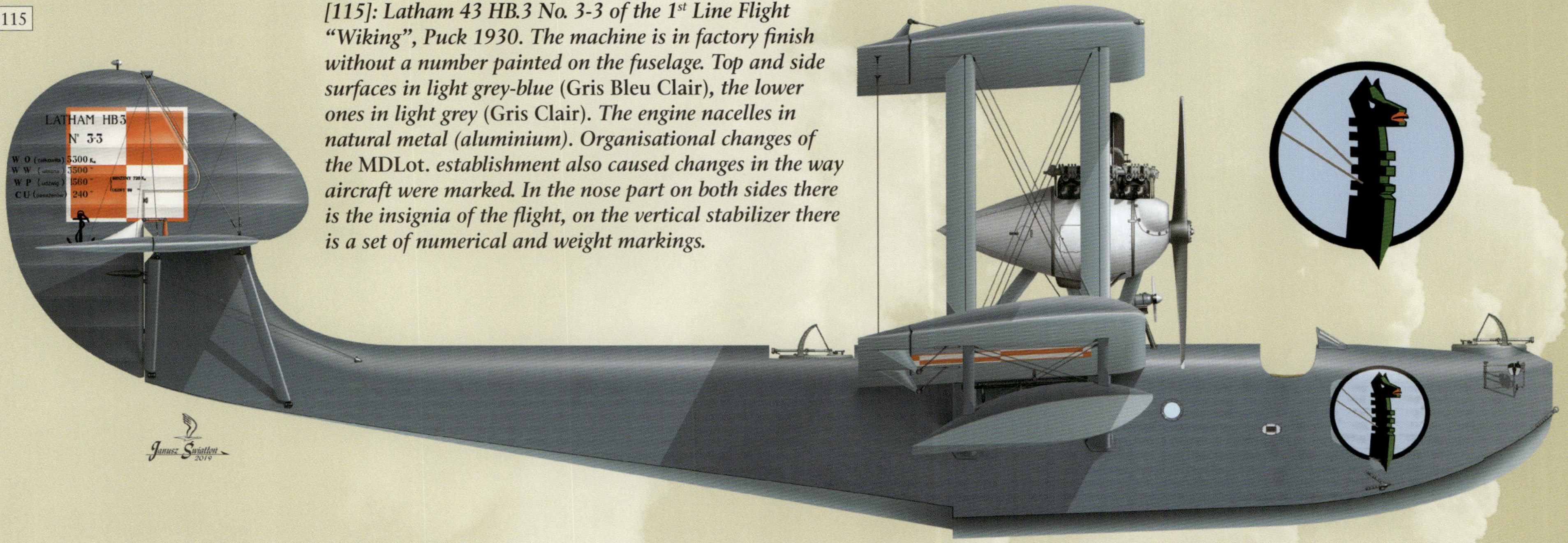

[115]: Latham 43 HB.3 No. 3-3 of the 1st Line Flight "Wiking", Puck 1930. The machine is in factory finish without a number painted on the fuselage. Top and side surfaces in light grey-blue (Gris Bleu Clair), *the lower ones in light grey* (Gris Clair). *The engine nacelles in natural metal (aluminium). Organisational changes of the MDLot. establishment also caused changes in the way aircraft were marked. In the nose part on both sides there is the insignia of the flight, on the vertical stabilizer there is a set of numerical and weight markings.*

116

*[116]: A colossus on the beach in Oksywie.
A Latham 43 HB.3 heavy flying boat of the 1st Line Flight "Wiking". Clearly visible are the flight emblem painted on the bow of the machine and the chequerboard with the inverted square layout. The chequerboard is also visible on the lower surface of the horizontal tail plane. (MOW in Hel)*

117

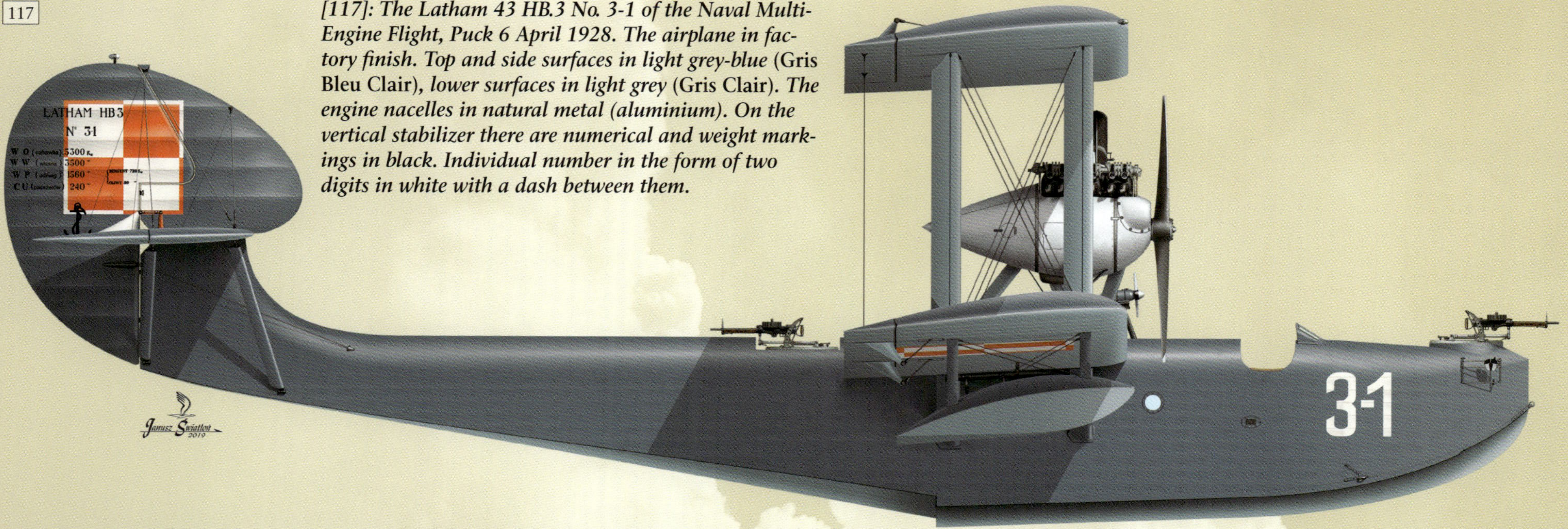

[117]: *The Latham 43 HB.3 No. 3-1 of the Naval Multi-Engine Flight, Puck 6 April 1928. The airplane in factory finish. Top and side surfaces in light grey-blue* (Gris Bleu Clair), *lower surfaces in light grey* (Gris Clair). *The engine nacelles in natural metal (aluminium). On the vertical stabilizer there are numerical and weight markings in black. Individual number in the form of two digits in white with a dash between them.*

118

[118]: Latham 43 HB.3 flying boat No. 3-1 photographed in the winter on the apron at the base in Puck. Attention is drawn to the early form of the aircraft number, with digits separated by a dash. In the background, on the left side, the harbour crane for servicing the flying boats. (Muzeum Lotnictwa Polskiego in Kraków)

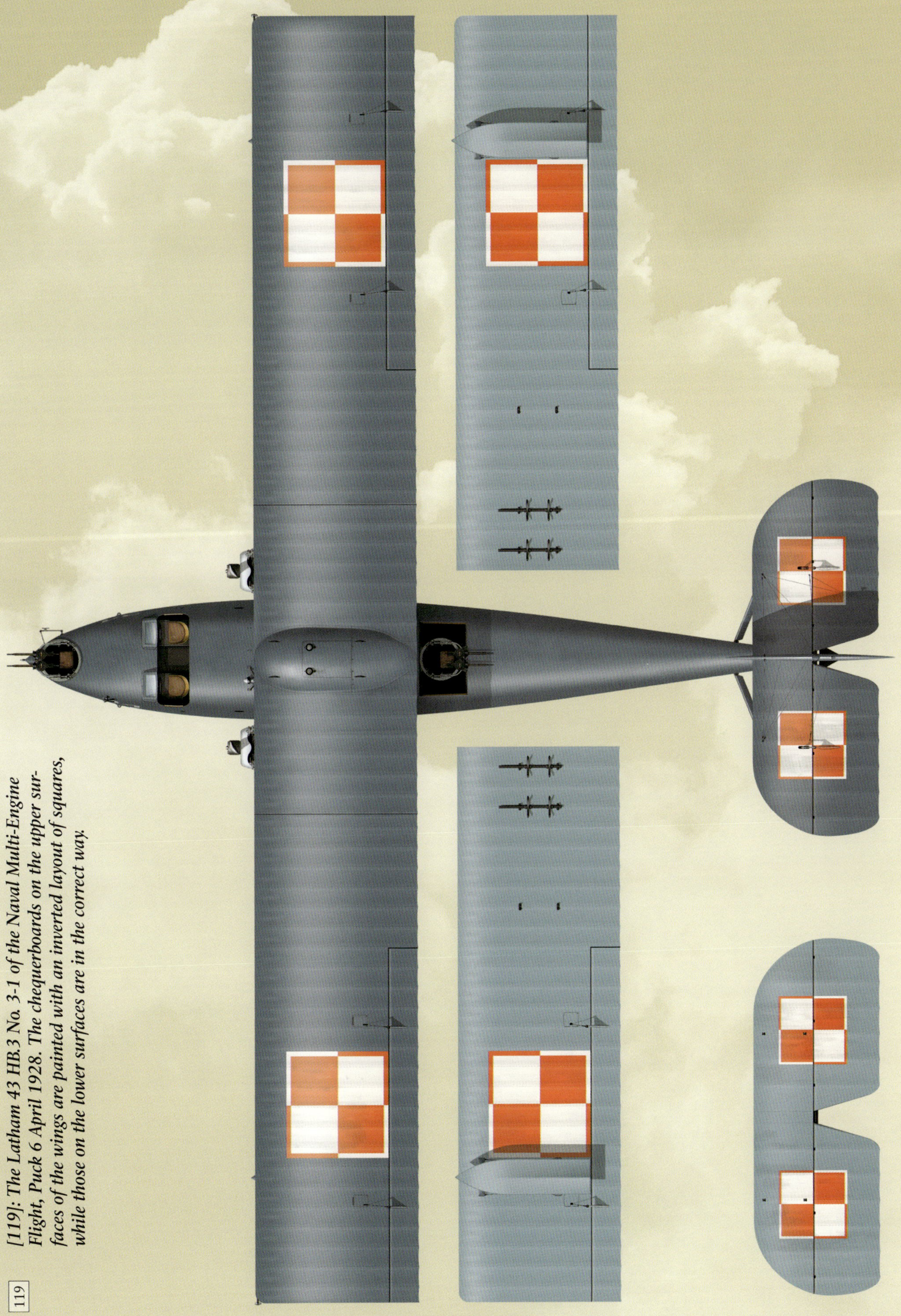

119

[119]: The Latham 43 HB.3 No. 3-1 of the Naval Multi-Engine Flight, Puck 6 April 1928. The chequerboards on the upper surfaces of the wings are painted with an inverted layout of squares, while those on the lower surfaces are in the correct way.

120

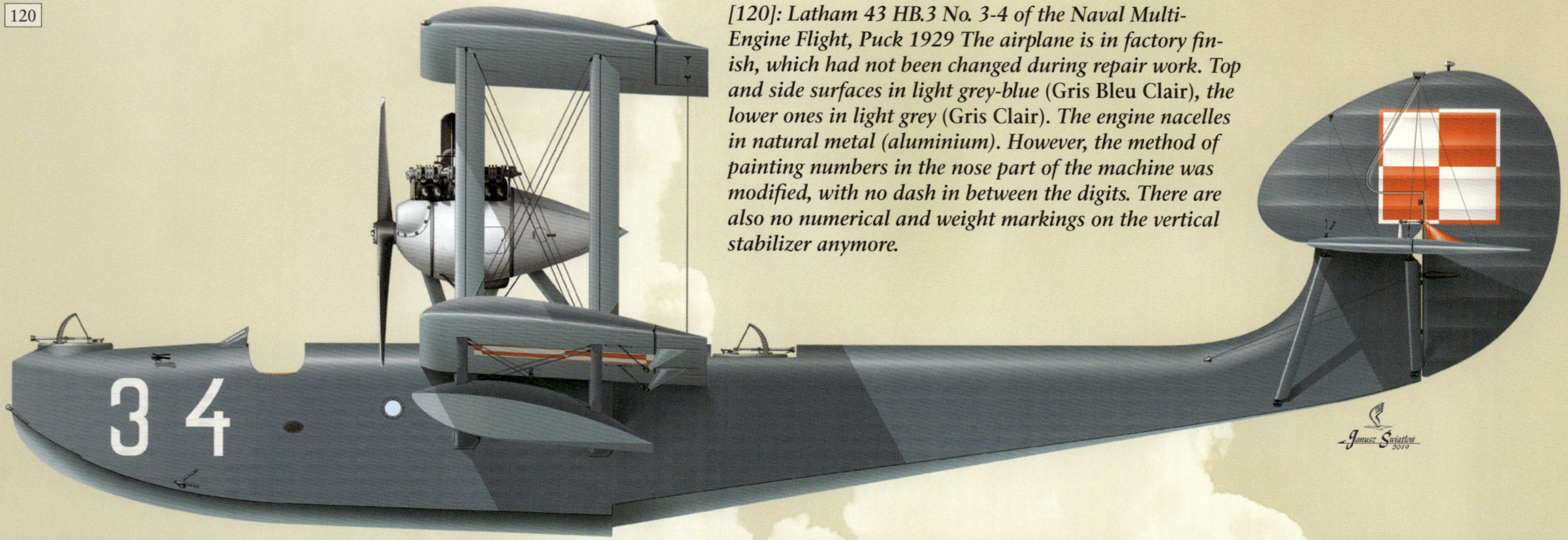

[120]: Latham 43 HB.3 No. 3-4 of the Naval Multi-Engine Flight, Puck 1929 The airplane is in factory finish, which had not been changed during repair work. Top and side surfaces in light grey-blue (Gris Bleu Clair)*, the lower ones in light grey* (Gris Clair)*. The engine nacelles in natural metal (aluminium). However, the method of painting numbers in the nose part of the machine was modified, with no dash in between the digits. There are also no numerical and weight markings on the vertical stabilizer anymore.*

121

122

[121–122]: Latham 43 HB.3 flying boats Nos. 35, 34, 37 in the air over the port in Gdynia. Under them there is the harbour named after Marshal Józef Piłsudski. The picture was taken by the Photographic Section of the Naval Air Squadron from Puck in the mid-1920s. (Muzeum Ziemi Puckiej)

123

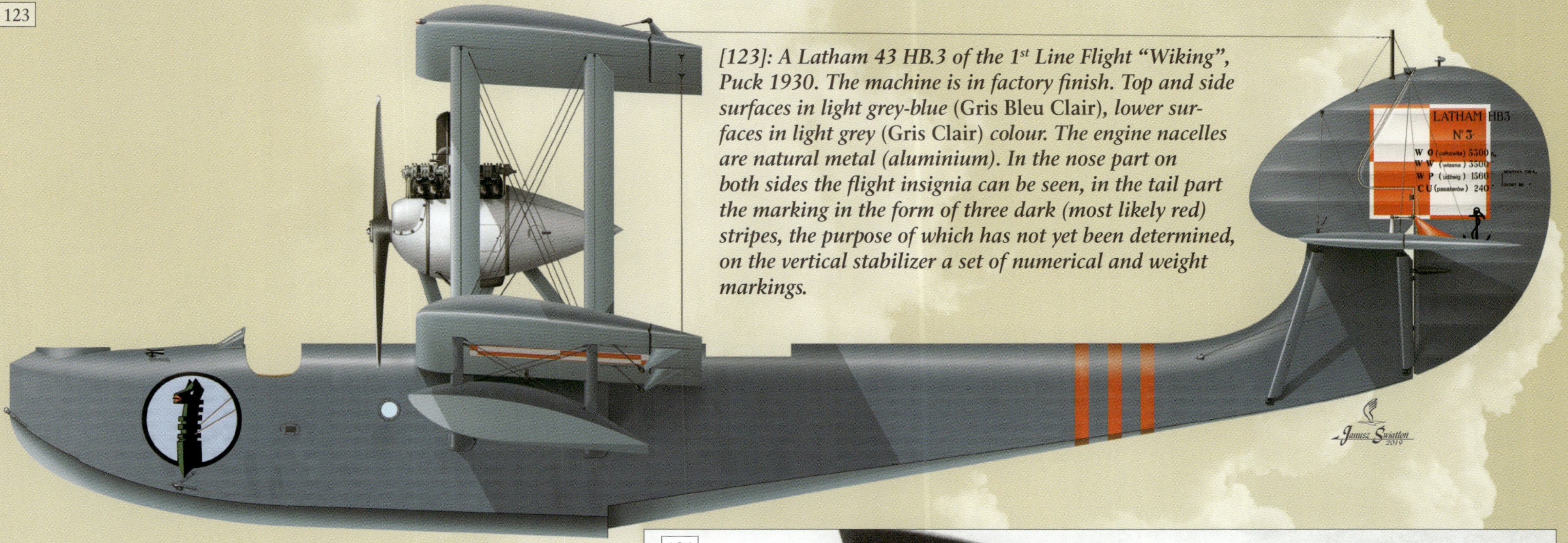

[123]: A Latham 43 HB.3 of the 1st Line Flight "Wiking", Puck 1930. The machine is in factory finish. Top and side surfaces in light grey-blue (Gris Bleu Clair)*, lower surfaces in light grey* (Gris Clair) *colour. The engine nacelles are natural metal (aluminium). In the nose part on both sides the flight insignia can be seen, in the tail part the marking in the form of three dark (most likely red) stripes, the purpose of which has not yet been determined, on the vertical stabilizer a set of numerical and weight markings.*

124

[124]: A Latham 43 HB.3 heavy flying boat of the 1st Line Flight "Wiking" set on a transport cart. On the bow, the emblem of the flight is visible. Three dark (red?) stripes are painted in the aft part of the fuselage. The chequerboards on the lower surfaces of the planes are properly painted, on the vertical stabilizer however, with the inverted layout of squares. (Wiesław Bączkowski archives from Stratus coll.)

SCHRECK FBA 17 HMT.2/HE.2

The most numerous group of French-manufactured aircraft used by the Polish naval aviation were the popular "Schrecks" or FBA 17s. They arrived in Poland in two variants, the HE.2 flying boat and the HMT.2 amphibious aircraft. Both were based on the same flying boat design with a biplane layout. Its designer was Ing. Luis Schreck, and the first prototype was made in 1924. Production was carried out by the FBA Hydravions Luis Schreck of Argentuil in the Seine Department. The FBA 17 proved to be a very successful design, used not only by the French naval aviation, but also exported to many countries around the world including Japan, Canada and the USA.

The fuselage was of boat style, wooden, truss construction, covered with plywood. It had a flat bottom and step, as well as a "moustache" for pushing waves aside. In the front part there was a two-seat, open crew cabin. The pilot occupied the space on the left, the observer sat on the right. Behind the cabin there was the wing chamber. The wings had a rectangular outline and a double-girder mixed construction covered with canvas. They were joined with metal struts, additionally stiffened with steel bracing wires. Only the upper panel was fitted with ailerons, while a pair of stabilizing floats were placed under the bottom one. The tail part was of a single, classic layout, covered with plywood, and the rudders with canvas. The horizontal stabiliser was additionally supported to the hull by metal struts. The drive was a 140 HP Hispano Suiza L4 straight engine or Hispano Suiza 8AB with an output of 180 HP. The engine was cooled with water, the radiator formed one block with the engine and was placed in the front of the engine nacelle. The nacelle itself was mounted in the classic way on trestles, in the central part of the wing chamber. The engine powered a two-blade, wooden pusher propeller. The FBA 17 in both versions did not have on-board weapons. Attempts were made to install a Vickers machine gun and, under the bottom panel, Alcan racks for four bombs weighing 12.5 kg each. The HE.2 flying boat also had the option of installing launchers for six smoke candles. Since aircraft of this variant were also used for training, they had dual control devices.

The amphibious HMT.2 was equipped with a two-wheeled chassis. It was placed under the lower panel and retracted into it with a manual mechanism, which was operated by the observer. In the tail part a fixed skid was mounted. The HMT.2s were equipped with a more powerful version of the engine i.e.

[125]: Three Schreck FBA 17 HE.2 aircraft (fore part of one of them is visible in the depths of the hangar) belonging to the Riverine Air Squadron in Pińsk. Also noteworthy is the unusual uniform of one of the sailors posing for the photo. The combination of white tunic and dark blue trousers was seldom seen in practice. The image is dated 1930. (Polish Navy Museum)

[126]: The wreckage of the Schreck FBA 17 HE.2 No. 4-5 flying boat being pulled ashore. Sailors are wearing white denim work uniforms. (Mariusz Konarski coll.)

127

128

[127]: Another opportunity for a commemorative photo. The flying boat Schreck FBA 17 HE.2 No. 4-3 by the beach in Hel. On the right, a second machine of this type is partially obscured by a group of vacationers. The breakwater of the naval port in Hel under construction is also visible. (MOW in Hel)

[128]: A group of officers posing for a photo by the Schreck FBA 17 HE.2 flying boat that was a part of the Training Flight. The clearly visible flight insignia is painted on the bow of the aircraft. Photograph was taken during the parachute training course for MDLot. personnel. Puck, 1929. (Mariusz Konarski coll.

[129]: The Schreck FBA 17 HE.2 flying boat No. 53 would later serve as the MDLot.'s commanding officer's personal machine. Until recently it was thought that it was the only aircraft of this type used during the war in September 1939. The picture comes from the period when the markings in the form of white large digits painted in the nose part of the fuselage, not separated by a dash were used, also there is the lack of inscriptions on the vertical stabilizer. The standard windshield was replaced with the type used on the amphibious HMT.2, which at that time had been decommissioned. (MOW in Hel)

129

the HS 8AB and a windscreen of more massive construction than in the case of the HE.2. Also, the fuel tank had a slightly larger capacity. In addition, it was possible to install an AVA on-board wireless set.

The order for these planes was placed in France in 1925. It was for six HE.2 flying boats and 12 amphibious HMT.2s, where 10 machines were purchased using funds from a loan and two were acquired from public contributions. Initially, these sported the civilian markings *Lubliniak*[1] and *L.O.P.P.* Puck's new aircraft were delivered by sea in 1926. Initially, they were assigned to the 1st Naval Observation Flight where the amphibians HMT.2 found themselves and the Training Section, which became the main user of the HE.2 flying boats. At the turn of 1928 and 1929, these aircraft were assigned to the Naval Observation Flight *(Morska Eskadra Obserwacyjna)*, Training Flight (*Eskadra Szkolna)* and the Riverine Air Platoon *(Rzeczny Pluton Lotniczy)* in Pińsk. In 1930–1931, most of the HMT.2 amphibians were taken over by the Riverine Air Platoon, later renamed the Riverine Air Squadron *(Rzeczna Eskadra Lotnicza)*, while all the HE.2 flying boats and several HMT.2 amphibians were assigned to the Training Flight (*Eskadra Szkolna*).

The FBA 17 aircraft in both versions should be considered successful designs. These aircraft were easy to fly and maintain. Therefore, they were used quite intensively for various tasks, mainly in the field of training.

The operational area of the Schreck FBA 17 aircraft was not limited only to the area of the Bay of Puck and the Polish coast. The compact design of these machines, which was ideally suited to take-offs and landings on lakes and rivers, and excellent flying properties meant that they performed flights whose destinations were places located at a considerable distance from Puck:

Domestic long-distance flights performed by the Schreck FBA 17 HMT.2 amphibians:

Date of departure	Aircraft No.	Route
1926	5-?	Puck – Janów – Puck
1926	5-?	Puck – Modlin – Puck
26 .05.1929	5-4	Puck – Toruń – Puck
19.07.1929	5-4	Puck – Grudziądz – Puck
27.08.1929	5-4	Puck – Starogard Gdański – Puck
19.10.1929	5-4	Puck – Świecie nad Wisłą – Puck
4.11.1929	5-4	Puck – Toruń – Puck
18.02.1930	5-10, 5-2, 5-4	Puck – Dęblin – Puck

The list should also be added to by propaganda flights carried out in 1926 by the civilian amphibian *Lubliniak*. During these flights, it landed, among other places, on the Bug River in Włodawa, the Wieprz River and also on the factory airfield of *Zakłady Mechaniczne Plage & Laśkiewicz* mechanical plant in Lublin. Similar flights were also performed by the second civilian amphibian – the *L.O.P.P.* However, no documents are currently known on the details of these flights.

Both types of Schreck FBA 17 machines were the basic flying equipment of the Riverine Air Platoon (from 1933, the Riverine Air Squadron), stationed in Pińsk. In 1926–1927, three machines were detached to the marshy area of Polesie in

1 A colloquial name of a local newspaper "Dziennik Lubelski", readers of which funded one of the machines.

130

[130]: The Schreck FBA 17 HMT.2 amphibious aircraft No. 54. Late variant of numbering. The lack of underwing floats is also noteworthy. (Polish Navy Museum)

131

[131]: In a moment we are letting go the anchor! The amphibian Schreck FBA 17 HMT.2 No. 5-7 on the water in the area of the naval base in Gdynia-Oksywie. This aircraft was part of the "Close Intelligence Flight" as this sub-unit was sometimes known. On 14 June 1929 it was crashed by Sgt. Jan Jeż during a landing at the port in Pińsk. (MOW in Hel)

order to carry out exercises, after which they returned to Puck. Upon formation of the Riverine Air Platoon, on 10 May 1928, three amphibians were transferred from Puck, and in the following years more of them. In total, three to six aircraft were stationed in Pińsk. The airplanes had to fly over 600 km on the Puck – Modlin – Warsaw – Brest – Pińsk route.

The Schreck FBA 17 HMT.2 amphibious aircraft performed intelligence, liaison and medical tasks. It is also known that one aircraft was used for spraying anti-mosquito and anti-malarial agents. Practical fire control of the Pińsk Riverine Flotilla *(Flotylla Pińska)* boats' guns was also carried out, as well as ground support from the air, which was more of a symbolic nature. At that time, attempts were made to mount a fixed weaponry on the Schreck FBA 17 HMT.2 amphibians. They were carried out at the turn of 1932 and 1933 by 2nd Lt. Wacław Marian Jurkiewicz and Ordnance Cpl. Bernard Hanuszewski. The latter remembered that:

"... I served with the Riverine Platoon in Pińsk from April 1932 until November 1933; my job was to mount and maintain weapons. At the turn of winter 1932/1933 2nd Lt. Wacław M. Jurkiewicz (observer) came up with the idea of trying to arm our amphibians with machine guns and suggested that I help him. Together, we drew a sketch of a Vickers machine gun mount and handed it over to the harbour workshop where it was made. We mounted this holder on one Schreck. In this way, we armed one amphibian (as far as I recall, initially during my stay in Pińsk, only one Schreck was in the platoon), which from then on performed flights already armed with one Vickers machine gun. In the workshop, mountings for the next amphibians were soon made, but the machine gun was permanently mounted on only one Schreck. It was transferred to another plane when the one on which it had been installed until then underwent repairs. In this way, the regularly transferred machine gun was in fact the armament of all three amphibians of the platoon. However, it was not enough for 2nd Lt. W. M. Jurkiewicz and he agreed by phone with the MDLot.'s *base in Puck, he asked for bomb racks to be sent to Pińsk. Soon, a train was sent from Puck carrying two French racks adapted to carry two POW bombs weighing 12.5 kg each. Both Alcan type racks I fitted under the lower plane on both sides of the fuselage of one of the amphibians"*[2].

This solution, however, only gave the illusion of the actual armament, because the fixed machine gun, shooting forward and operated by the observer, was ineffective and dangerous at the same time, because the observer had to lean overboard when firing, which obviously threatened that he could fall out of the airplane. There is also no information on the use of armed bombs. However, training bombs of the same weight but with concrete filling were used.

The Riverine Air Squadron ceased to exist on 20 December 1937. Some of the personnel and Schreck FBA 17 HMT.2 amphibians were sent by rail to Puck. In Pińsk up until 1938 there was one more amphibian remaining (according to some sources, two).

The Schreck FBA 17 airplanes, although popular among the pilots, were notorious for the largest number of accidents, including fatal crashes. However, this resulted from their intensive use, it was in no case caused by the defective construction of the aircraft itself.

On 23 May 1927, during a training flight over the Bay of Puck, amphibious aircraft No. 5-1 crashed. It was flying over one of the beaches of the Hel Peninsula in the region of Jastarnia. The pilot decided to show off and perform a series of acrobatic manoeuvres for the holiday-makers down on the beach. During this show, he caught the wing against some trees and fell to the ground. Cpt. Jan Kazimierz Malicki died, while the mechanic Cpl. Ireneusz Sawostianik was seriously injured. Here is the account of one of the sons who recreated the memories of his father:

"It was a good flying day, the holiday season was already in full swing and the beaches were full of people. Cpt. Malicki wanted to show off his aerobatics, which was very fashionable then and he performed a barrel roll. At the end of this manoeuvre, the engine stopped working and the machine went into a dive. The pilot could not level the machine, because the event took place only a few hundred metres above the Hel Peninsula. Just above the ground the pilot tried to bail out with his parachute, but it did not open and Cpt. Malicki was killed when he hit some trees. Our father did not try to bail out because he did not have a parachute. The machine hit the trees at high speed, cut off some tops, and finally due the resistance of the branches turned on its back, with its tail hitting the water. The mechanic hung with his head down just over the water. He was saved by fishermen from Kuźnica, who saw the impact and sailed from the shore. He stayed in hospital broken and injured for nearly half a year, after which he returned to service. The pilot's body was found among the trees of the peninsula, and the whole event took place between Chałupy and Kuźnica"[3]. The event described above was the first accident involving a French production aircraft that took place in Naval Air Squadron *(MDLot.)* in Puck. It is no wonder that this event

2 Andrzej Olejko, "Lotnictwo Morskie II Rzeczypospolitej", Wyd. ZP Grupa, Warsaw, 2010, p. 231

3 Andrzej Olejko, "Lotnictwo Morskie II Rzeczypospolitej", Wyd. ZP Grupa, Warsaw, 2010, p. 188.

had wide repercussions, not only at the *MDLot.'s* base, but also on the whole of the coastal area.

The day of 5 July 1928 brought another accident. During a night landing Lt. Hilary Wysocki crashed seaplane No. 4-5. Also, aircraft No. 4-6 was broken down, which must have to take place before 1929 because this machine is not shown in the records of aircraft from this year.

On 14 June 1929, an accident occurred at the river harbour in Pińsk when during a landing on the Pina River plane No. 5-7 was destroyed.

Another disaster took place on 5 December 1929. During a landing on the Bay of Puck at dusk and the occurrence of the *glada*[4] phenomenon, flying boat No. 4-1 was completely wrecked. This phenomenon is characteristic only for the basin of the Bay of Puck. In the absence of wind and in foggy air as well as the smooth surface of the water, the horizon line disappears. The pilot of an aircraft in the air could see the bottom of the shallow bay waters, but he could not see the surface of the water and could not properly assess the height when approaching the landing. On that day, the crew consisting of Lt. Kazimierz Szalewicz and 2nd Lt. Zygmunt Kawęcki-Dołęga were returning from Gdynia, while the duties of the flight control officer at the base in Puck were performed by Lt. Adolf Stempowski. Having observed that *glada* had formed on the Bay, he agreed with the base in Oksywie, that the crew would stay there overnight and return to Puck only the next day. It turned out, however, that the flying boat was already in the air and soon appeared over the Bay. Stempowski knew what would happen. The Schreck landed with too much force and smashed against the surface of the water, the pilot, due to *glada*, incorrectly assessed the altitude. As a result of the accident, 2nd Lt. Zygmunt Kawcęki-Dołęga hit his head against the instrument panel, lost consciousness and drowned, while Lt. Kazimierz Szalewicz was injured. The plane was completely destroyed and consequently written off from the unit's records.

11 April 1930 is the date of the next disaster. During the first flight right after its renovation, No. 4-3 flying boat's engine failed. The airplane was located over the Bay of Puck at an altitude of 600 metres. The engine stopped working, as a result of which the machine fell into an uncontrolled spin and fell into the sea. The crew of Lt. Zygmunt Majewski and Cpl. Bernard Łukaszyk died on the spot. The consequence of this event was an order issued on 13 April 1930 by the *MDLot.'s* HQ, according to which a permanent commission was appointed to check the technical condition of aircraft returning to service after periodic repairs. As a result of the work of this commission, a number of design flaws were detected, which resulted in the order to ban flights on all Schreck FBA 17s. This order was cancelled only in April 1931.

On 5 May 1931. during landing, one of the Training Flight's *(Eskadra Szkolna)* machines was damaged. However, there is no certain information on the number of this aircraft, but it is known that the pilot was Lt. Bronisław Lubińkowski.

The last accident took place on 11 August 1931. when the landing gear was damaged, most likely it was machine No. 5-5.

During their service on the Polish coast, the Schreck crews also carried out one combat flight. On 16 March 1930 machine No. 5-11 took off from Puck in order to intercept a German Junkers F-13W aircraft (No. D-1048), which was trying to encroach on Polish territorial waters. The intruder was spotted by the amphibian's crew, already on the surface of the water, moving westwards. The German plane did not react. The reason most probably was the fact that the German machine carried some weapons on board and did not want to provoke an incident.

Most Schreck FBA 17 machines were decommissioned in the first half of the 1930s. The reason was the machine's

4 "Mirror" in the Kashubian dialect.

[132]: Almost everyone who spent their holidays at the Polish seaside before the war could take a closer look at a machine of the Naval Air Squadron from Puck. In this photograph a group of holidaymakers vacationing on the beach in Hel are watching the Schreck FBA 17 HMT.2 amphibious plane No. 57. (MOW in Hel)

132

133

[133]: The Schreck FBA 17 HMT.2 amphibian No. 51 crashed on 23 May 1927 on the beach between Chałupy and Kuźnica. The reason was engine failure when performing aerobatics, which the pilot decided to demonstrate to the vacationers. Cpt. Jan K. Malicki died while Junior Craftsman Ireneusz Sawostianik suffered serious injuries. (Muzeum Ziemi Puckiej)

134

[134]: Seamen of the MDLot. *and Kashubian fishermen at the wreckage of the Schreck FBA 17 HMT.2 amphibious aircraft which crashed on 23 May 1927 in the Kuźnica area. (Muzeum Ziemi Puckiej)*

135

[135]: FBA 17 HE.2 flying boat No. 43 was destroyed on 11 April 1930. In the crash, 2nd Lt. Zygmunt Majewski and Junior Crafstman Bernard Łukasik both perished. The accident happened during a flight over the Bay of Puck, when an engine failure occurred. (Muzeum Ziemi Puckiej)

[136]: Wreckage of the FBA 17 HE.2 flying boat No. 41. The accident took place on 5 December 1929. 2nd Lt. Zygmunt Kawęcki-Dołęga was killed. The crash was caused by the glada phenomenon. (Muzeum Ziemi Puckiej)

136

wear with a service life set at five years. Until the outbreak of the war in the records of the *MDLot.* there were two Schreck FBA 17s – No. 4-4 having been the executive aircraft of the *MDLot.'s* commanding officer and a plane with the mysterious number 4-0. According to orders, upon commencement of military operations, together with other flying equipment, they were evacuated from Puck to Hel and anchored there near the military port. Both Schrecks were destroyed as a result of the German seaplane raids on 8 September 1939, thus ending the history of French aircraft in Polish naval aviation.

Periods of service and assignments of the FBA Schreck HE.2 flying boats

Type	No.	Delivered	Assignments within the *MDLot.*	Written off	Notes
Schreck FBA 17 HE.2	4-1	1926	1926–1929 – Training Section	5.12.1929	Destroyed when landing. Lt. Zygmunt Dołęga – Kawęcki died.
Schreck FBA 17 HE.2	4-2	1926	1926–1928 – Training Section 1928 – Naval Multi-Engine Flight 1928–1933 – Training Flight 1934 – *MDLot.* HQ Platoon 1934–1939 – Training Platoon	8.09.1939	Destroyed in September 1939 at Stary Hel
Schreck FBA 17 HE.2	4-3	1926	1926–1928 – Training Section/*MDLot.'s* reserve 1929 – Naval Observation Flight, 1929–1930 – Training Section/workshops	11.04.1930	Destroyed during forced landing on the Bay of Puck. 2nd Lt. Zygmunt Majewski and Cpl. Bernard Łukasik died
Schreck FBA 17 HE.2	4-4	1926	1926–1928 – Training Section/*MDLot.'s* reserve 1929–1933 – Naval Observation Flight 1933–1934 – *MDLot.* HQ Platoon 1935–1937 – Riverine Air Squadron 1937–1939 – HQ Platoon, *MDLot.'s* officer commanding machine	8.09.1939	Destroyed in September 1939 at Stary Hel
Schreck FBA 17 HE.2	4-5	1926	1926–1928 – Training Section	5.07.1928	Destroyed after crash landing on 5.07.1928.
Schreck FBA 17 HE.2	4-6	1926	*MDLot.'s* reserve	31.05.1926	Spare parts magazine for Nos. 4-2 and 4-4

137

[137]: Polesie marshes! The Schreck FBA 17 HMT.2 amphibian No. 5-2 with a container of insecticide fitted to its side. (Tomasz J. Kopański coll.)

138

[138]: The riverine port in Pińsk. The Schreck FBA 17 HMT.2 amphibious aircraft No. 58 on the crane. In the background the boats of the Pińsk Flotilla can be seen. (Tomasz J. Kopański coll.)

Periods of service and assignments of the Schreck FBA 17 HMT.2 amphibians

Type	No.	Delivered	Assignments within the *MDLot.*	Written off	Notes
Schreck FBA 17 HMT.2	5-1	1926	1926–1927 – Naval Observation Flight	23.05.1927	Crashed in the area of Jastarnia on the Hel Peninsula. Cpt. Jan Majewski killed
Schreck FBA 17 HMT.2	5-2	1926	1926–1927 – Naval Observation Flight 1927–1928 – Riverine Air Platoon 1929–1930 – Training Section, 1930–1936 – Riverine Air Squadron	27–28.02.1936	Crashed on 30.08.1935. Until written off the wreckage was stored at the Riverine Air Squadron workshops in Pińsk
Schreck FBA 17 HMT.2	5-3	1926	1926–1927 – Naval Observation Flight 1927 – Riverine Air Platoon 1927–1929 – Naval Observation Flight 1929–1937 – Riverine Air Platoon/Riverine Air Squadron	01.1938	-
Schreck FBA 17 HMT.2	5-4	1926	1926–1927 – Naval Observation Flight 1927 – Riverine Air Platoon 1927–1929 – Naval Observation Flight 1930–1937 – Riverine Air Squadron 1937 – at the Puck base (no data on its exact assignment)	No data available	-
Schreck FBA 17 HMT.2	5-5	1926	1926–1929 – Naval Observation Flight 1929 – Riverine Air Platoon	No data available	-
Schreck FBA 17 HMT.2	5-6	1926	1926–1929 – Naval Observation Flight 1929 – Riverine Air Platoon 1929–1933 – at Puck (no data on the exact assignment) 1933–1936 – Riverine Air Squadron	27–28.02.1936	-
Schreck FBA 17 HMT.2	5-7	1926	1926–1929 – Naval Observation Flight 1929 – Riverine Air Platoon	27–28.02.1936	Crashed during take-off on the Pina River on 14.06.1935
Schreck FBA 17 HMT.2	5-8	1926	1926–1928 – Naval Observation Flight 1928 – Riverine Air Platoon 1928–1929 – *MDLot.* workshops 1929 – Riverine Air Platoon 1929–1936 – at Puck (no data on the exact assignment) 1936–1937 – Riverine Air Squadron	28.12.1937	-
Schreck FBA 17 HMT.2	5-9	1926	1926–1929 – *MDLot.'s* reserve 1929 – Riverine Air Platoon 1929–1936 – at Puck (no data on the exact assignment) 1936–1937 – Riverine Air Squadron	12.1937	-
Schreck FBA 17 HMT.2	5-10	1926	1926–1929 – Training Section 1929 – Riverine Air Platoon 1929–1936 – at Puck (no data on the exact assignment) 1936–1937 – Riverine Air Squadron	12.1937	-
Schreck FBA 17 HMT.2	511	1926	1926–1930 – in civilian use 1930–1935 – Training Flight 1935–1936 – Riverine Air Squadron	27–28.02.1936	"Lubliniak"
Schreck FBA 17 HMT.2	512	1926	1926–1927 – in civilian use 1927 – in the 4th Dept. of the Air Force reserve	No data available	"L.O.P.P."

139

[139]: Somewhere on the Pripyat River. The Schreck FBA 17 HMT.2 amphibian No. 5-4 moored to the bank. Note the folded landing gear as well as the absence of the grille from the front part of the engine nacelle. (Tomasz J. Kopański coll.)

140

[140]: The Schreck FBA 17 HE.2 No. 4-4, Naval Observation Flight, Puck, 1929. The machine is in factory finish. Upper surfaces of fuselage, planes and horizontal fins in blue-grey (Gris Bleu Foncé), *lower and side surfaces in light grey-blue* (Gris Bleu Clair). *The fuselage below the waterline is covered with a dark grey waterproofing agent* (Gris Foncé). *The engine nacelle is in the colour of the upper surfaces, while the trestle on which it rests as well as the struts are in the lower surfaces' colour. Markings in the form of digits separated by a dash. On the vertical stabilizer the type designation and a set of numerical and weight markings in black.*

[141]: The Schreck FBA 17 HE.2 flying boat No. 4-4 photographed by the beach in Hel. The inscription placed in the picture suggests it was taken in 1929. At that time, the early markings scheme was in force, both digits were separated by a dash. The airplane is in the standard French camouflage pattern. In the background construction work at the naval port in Hel can be seen. (Muzeum Ziemi Puckiej)

141

142

[142]: The FBA 17 HE.2 flying boat No. 4-4. In a leather jacket is Lt. Adolf Stempkowski. The photo was taken at the base in Puck in 1928. (Muzeum Ziemi Puckiej)

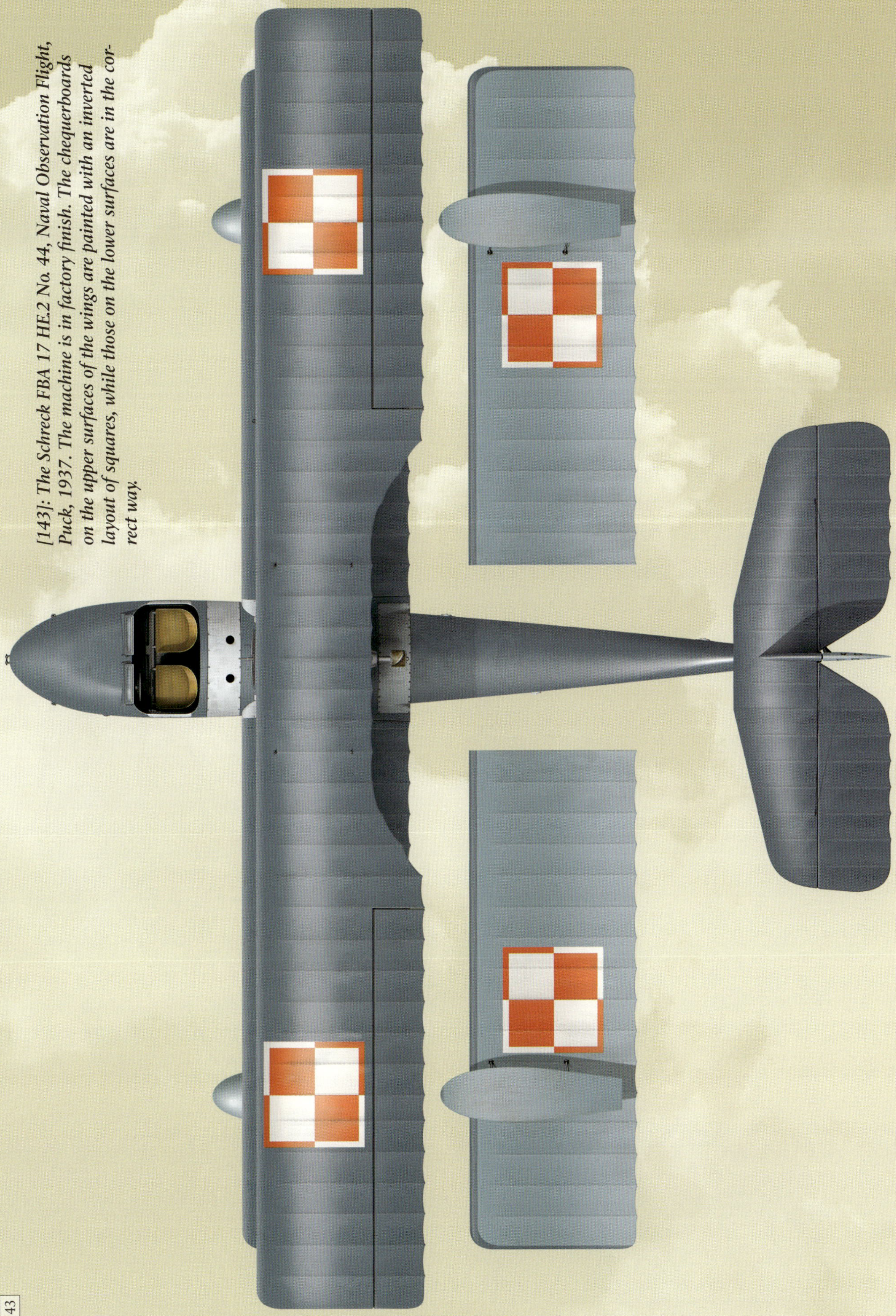

143

[143]: The Schreck FBA 17 HE.2 No. 44, Naval Observation Flight, Puck, 1937. The machine is in factory finish. The chequerboards on the upper surfaces of the wings are painted with an inverted layout of squares, while those on the lower surfaces are in the correct way.

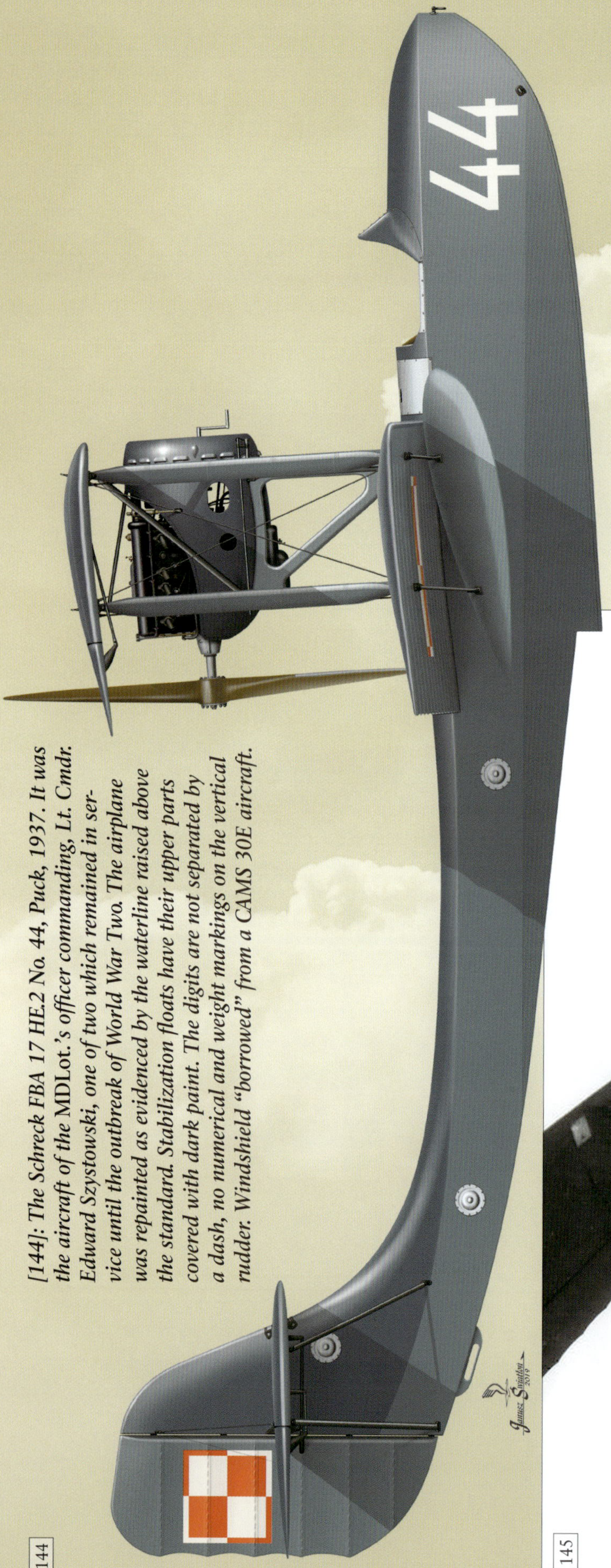

144

[144]: *The Schreck FBA 17 HE.2 No. 44, Puck, 1937. It was the aircraft of the MDLot.'s officer commanding, Lt. Cmdr. Edward Szystowski, one of two which remained in service until the outbreak of World War Two. The airplane was repainted as evidenced by the waterline raised above the standard. Stabilization floats have their upper parts covered with dark paint. The digits are not separated by a dash, no numerical and weight markings on the vertical rudder. Windshield "borrowed" from a CAMS 30E aircraft.*

145

[145]: The Schreck FBA 17 HE.2 flying boat No. 44, later served as the MDLot. commander's machine. Until recently it had been thought that it was the only aircraft of this type used in September 1939. The image comes from the period when the markings in the form of digits painted in the nose part of the fuselage were not separated by a dash, there are no inscriptions on the fin either. The standard windshield was replaced with the type used previously in the CAMS 30E flying boats, which at that time had already been decommissioned. (MOW in Hel)

146

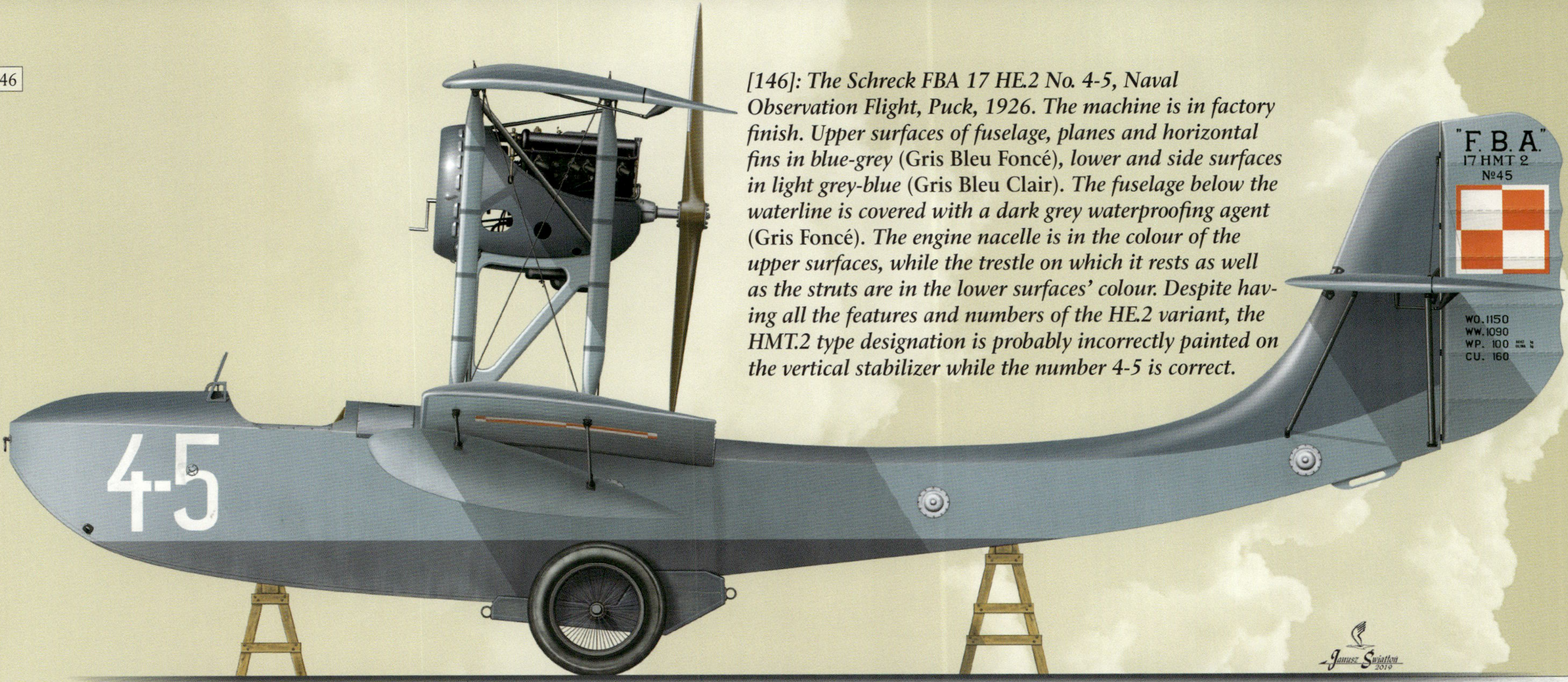

[146]: The Schreck FBA 17 HE.2 No. 4-5, Naval Observation Flight, Puck, 1926. The machine is in factory finish. Upper surfaces of fuselage, planes and horizontal fins in blue-grey (Gris Bleu Foncé), *lower and side surfaces in light grey-blue* (Gris Bleu Clair). *The fuselage below the waterline is covered with a dark grey waterproofing agent* (Gris Foncé). *The engine nacelle is in the colour of the upper surfaces, while the trestle on which it rests as well as the struts are in the lower surfaces' colour. Despite having all the features and numbers of the HE.2 variant, the HMT.2 type designation is probably incorrectly painted on the vertical stabilizer while the number 4-5 is correct.*

147

[147]: Schreck FBA 17 HE.2 flying boat No. 4-5 being pulled ashore on the slipway at MDLot. *base in Puck. The lightweight design of this aircraft allowed it to be brought ashore without the use of a harbour crane. Clearly visible are the colour division lines on the fuselage and planes as well as the early form of marking, i.e. 4-5. In the background on the left, the village of Swarzewo can be seen. (MOW in Hel)*

148

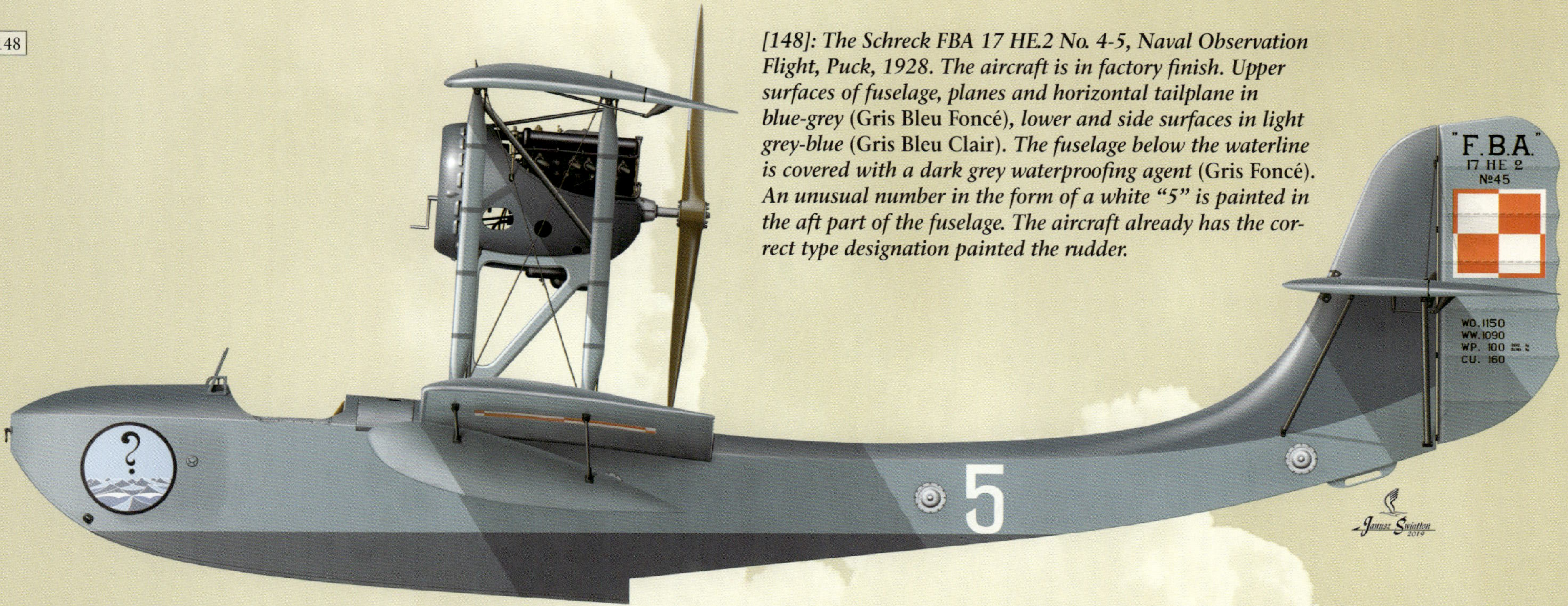

[148]: The Schreck FBA 17 HE.2 No. 4-5, Naval Observation Flight, Puck, 1928. The aircraft is in factory finish. Upper surfaces of fuselage, planes and horizontal tailplane in blue-grey (Gris Bleu Foncé), *lower and side surfaces in light grey-blue* (Gris Bleu Clair). *The fuselage below the waterline is covered with a dark grey waterproofing agent* (Gris Foncé). *An unusual number in the form of a white "5" is painted in the aft part of the fuselage. The aircraft already has the correct type designation painted the rudder.*

149 *[149–150]: Wreckage of the Schreck FBA 17 HE.2 flying boat No. 4-5, crashed during landing on the Bay of Puck on 11 August 1931. The machine was piloted by Lt. Hilary Wysocki. Note the "5" painted in a non-standard way in the aft part of the fuselage. (Mariusz Konarski coll.)*

150

151

[151]: The Schreck FBA 17 HE.2 No. 4-4, MDLot. *Training Flight, Puck, 1930. The machine is in factory finish. Upper surfaces of fuselage, planes and horizontal tailplane in blue-grey* (Gris Bleu Foncé), *lower and side surfaces in light grey-blue* (Gris Bleu Clair). *The fuselage below the waterline is covered with a dark grey waterproofing agent* (Gris Foncé). *Engine nacelle is in the colour of the upper surfaces, while the trestle on which it rests as well as the struts are in the lower surface colour. The number in the form oof a white "4" is painted in the rear part of the fuselage, the insignia of the Training Flight were painted on both sides in the fore part of the fuselage.*

152

[152–153]: The Schreck FBA 17 HE.2 flying boat No. 4-4 having just landed on the Bay of Puck. In the background the Hel Peninsula is visible. On the left stands Leading Hand R. Urbaniak. Attention is drawn to the Training Flight's insignia on the nose of the aircraft, and No. 4 painted in the aft part of the fuselage as well as the folded winsdcreen. (Mariusz Konarski coll.)

153

154 *[154]: The Schreck FBA 17 HE.2 No. 40, Puck, August, 1939. The machine is in factory finish, one of two aircraft of this type that survived in active service until the outbreak of war. Upper surfaces of fuselage, wings and horizontal tailplane are in blue-grey* (Gris Bleu Foncé), *lower and side surfaces in light grey-blue* (Gris Bleu Clair). *The fuselage below the waterline is black* (noir).

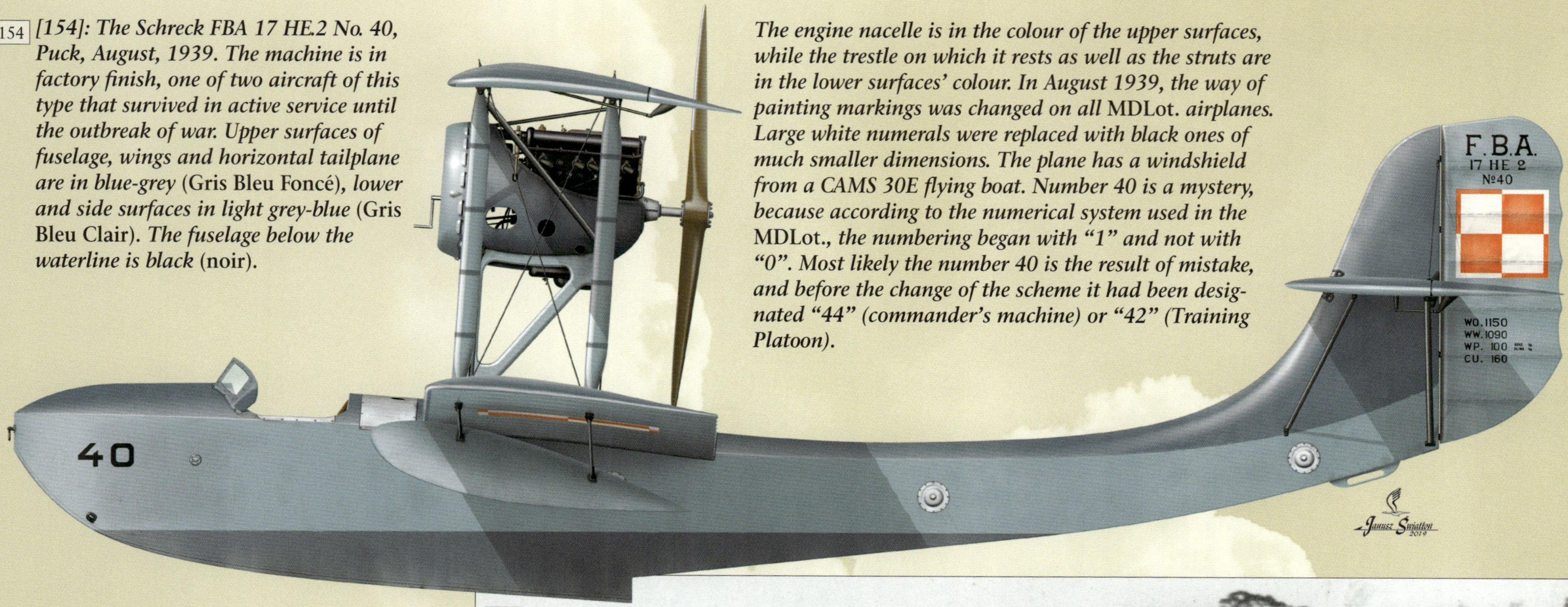

The engine nacelle is in the colour of the upper surfaces, while the trestle on which it rests as well as the struts are in the lower surfaces' colour. In August 1939, the way of painting markings was changed on all MDLot. *airplanes. Large white numerals were replaced with black ones of much smaller dimensions. The plane has a windshield from a CAMS 30E flying boat. Number 40 is a mystery, because according to the numerical system used in the* MDLot., *the numbering began with "1" and not with "0". Most likely the number 40 is the result of mistake, and before the change of the scheme it had been designated "44" (commander's machine) or "42" (Training Platoon).*

155

[155]: Wreckage of Schreck FBA 17 HE.2 flying boat No. 4-0. The photograph was taken in the area of Stary Hel, most probably in October 1939 as evidenced by the summer uniforms of the German seamen posing for this image. Clearly visible are the colour division lines. It is also worth paying attention to one detail of the construction of both Schrecks Nos. 4-0 and 4-4. Both machines had windshields "borrowed" from the CAMS 30E flying boats, which at that time had been withdrawn from service. This windshield was of much more solid structure and protected the crew better against wind and bad weather, however, its mounting had to be adapted to the construction of the FBA 17 cockpit. (Wawrzyniec Markowski coll.)

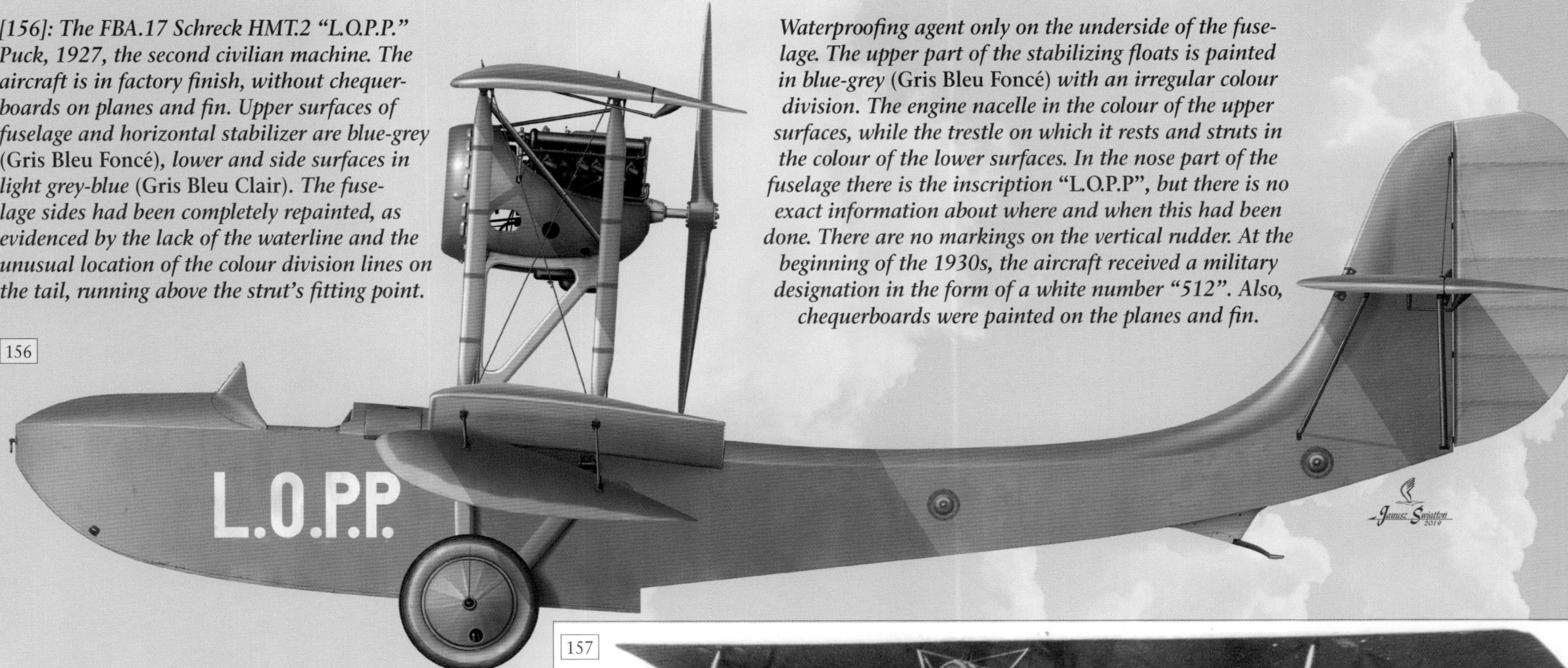

156

[156]: The FBA.17 Schreck HMT.2 "L.O.P.P." Puck, 1927, the second civilian machine. The aircraft is in factory finish, without chequerboards on planes and fin. Upper surfaces of fuselage and horizontal stabilizer are blue-grey (Gris Bleu Foncé), *lower and side surfaces in light grey-blue* (Gris Bleu Clair). *The fuselage sides had been completely repainted, as evidenced by the lack of the waterline and the unusual location of the colour division lines on the tail, running above the strut's fitting point.*

Waterproofing agent only on the underside of the fuselage. The upper part of the stabilizing floats is painted in blue-grey (Gris Bleu Foncé) *with an irregular colour division. The engine nacelle in the colour of the upper surfaces, while the trestle on which it rests and struts in the colour of the lower surfaces. In the nose part of the fuselage there is the inscription* "L.O.P.P", *but there is no exact information about where and when this had been done. There are no markings on the vertical rudder. At the beginning of the 1930s, the aircraft received a military designation in the form of a white number "512". Also, chequerboards were painted on the planes and fin.*

157

[157]: The FBA.17 Schreck HMT.2 amphibian "L.O.P.P". *(Robert Gretzyngier coll.)*

158

[158]: The Schreck FBA 17 HMT.2 No. 4-5, Training Flight, Puck, 1930. The airplane is in factory finish, unchanged during periodic repairs. Upper surfaces of fuselage, planes and horizontal stabilizers in blue-grey (Gris Bleu Foncé), *bottom and side surfaces in light grey-blue* (Gris Bleu Clair), *fuselage below the waterline in black* (noir). *The engine nacelle in natural metal (aluminium). On the nose part, on both sides, the Training Flight insignia are painted. Instead of a white number, three dark (most likely red) stripes on the aft part of the fuselage.*

159

160

[159–160]: The FBA 17 Schreck HMT.2 amphibian anchored somewhere in the rushes of the Płótnica River. The machine belonged to the Training Flight, as evidenced by the emblem painted on the nose of the fuselage. In the rear part of the fuselage there are three thin stripes painted in a dark colour, most likely red. What their meaning was is not known. Also noteworthy is the Venturi nozzle, fi tted atypically on the right side of the windshield. (Polish Aviation Museum, Kraków)

[161]: The Schreck FBA 17 HMT.2 No. 4-5, Training Flight, Puck, 1930. The chequerboards on the upper surfaces of the wings are painted with an inverted layout of squares, while those on the lower surfaces are in the correct way.

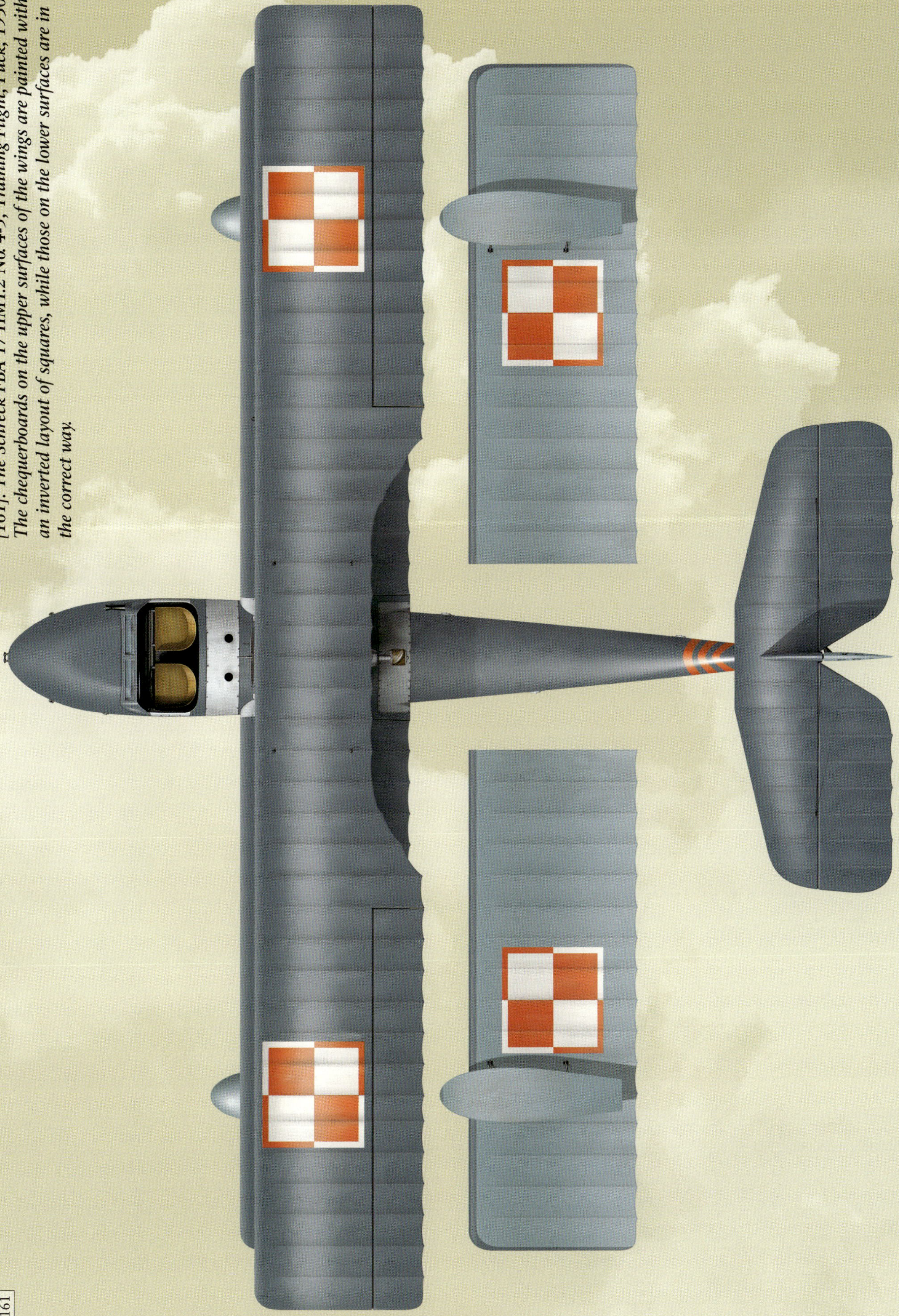

161

[162]: The Schreck FBA 17 HMT.2 "Lubliner By The Readers Of Voice Of Lublin" (Lubliniak Czytelników Głosu Lubelskiego), *Lublin, 1926. The aircraft is in factory finish, however, with some changes when compared to the original pattern. Upper surfaces of fuselage, planes and horizontal stabilizers are blue-grey (*Gris Bleu Foncé*), bottom and side surfaces in light grey-blue (*Gris Bleu Clair*). The sides had probably been repainted as indicated by the irregular waterline at the front and an the unusual course of the colour division on the tail.*

The bottom of the hull had been repainted too, as indicated by the lack of a darker colour of the waterline visible on one of the other photos. The front part of the engine nacelle is painted in a darker colour. Since it was originally a civilian machine, it did not sport the chequerboards painted on the planes and fin, on the latter only the type designation and a small black anchor were painted. In the nose part, a white foundation inscription and the FBA logo were painted. Also the latter had been modified. Originally, the pennant should be blue/white/red, while in the image it is clearly visible that it is left in one colour. Maybe it was done in order to avoid the foreign national colours in the machine's set of markings.

162

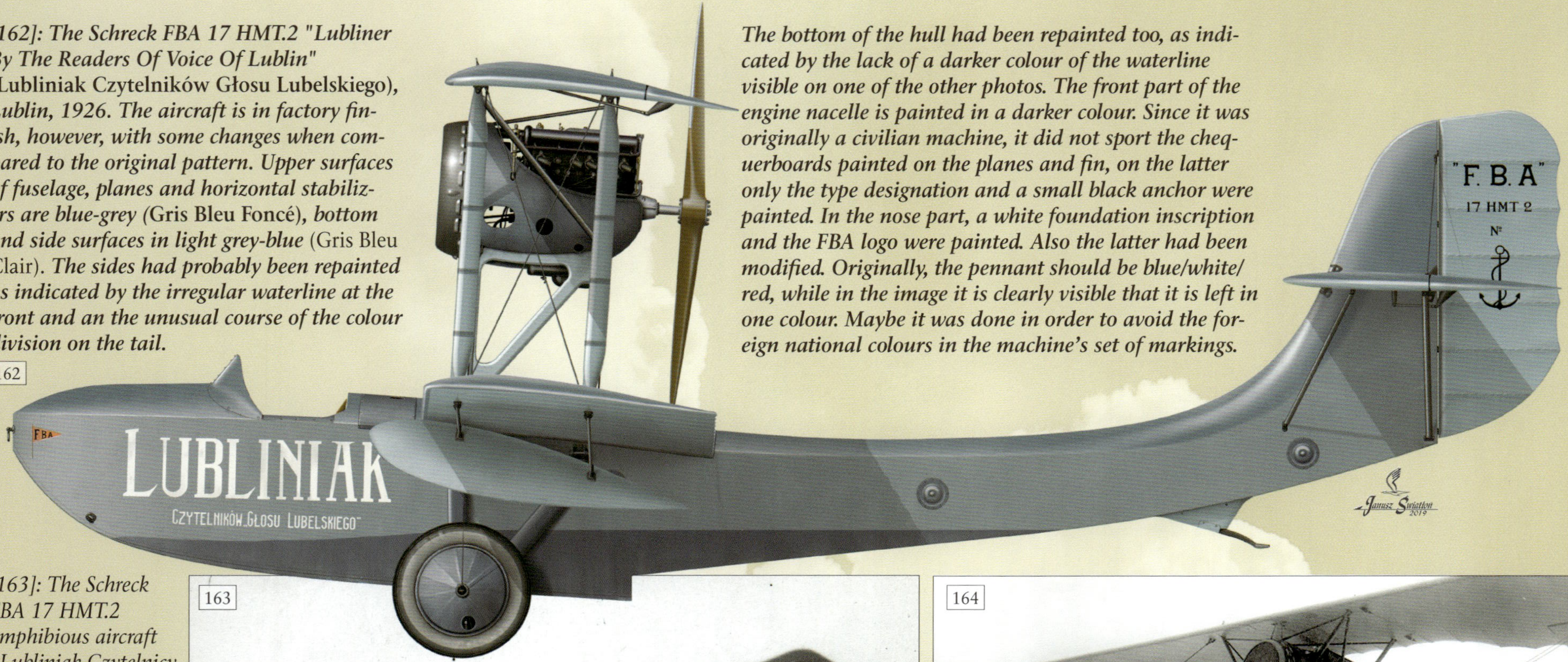

163

[163]: The Schreck FBA 17 HMT.2 amphibious aircraft "Lubliniak Czytelnicy Głosu Lubelskiego". The differences in painting in relation to the adopted standards in the form of the irregular waterline can be observed, as well as the unusual colour distribution on the tail, waterproofing agent on the bottom part of the fuselage painted over and the front engine nacelle painted with a clearly darker colour. (MOW in Hel)

164

[164]: The Schreck FBA 17 HMT.2 "Lubliniak Czytelnicy Głosu Lubelskiego". Clearly visible are the foundation inscription and the FBA logo. At that time, the airplane did not sport chequerboards. They appeared only after the military took over the machine and assigned it the number "511". (Polish Aviation Museum, Kraków)

165

[165]: *The Schreck FBA 17 HMT.2 No. 511, Puck, 1930. This is the former “Lubliniak” with military numbering and the chequerboards painted with the reversed order of fields. The aircraft was repainted as evidenced by the way the waterline is painted and the darker hue of the rudder.*

[166–167]: *The Schreck FBA 17 HMT.2, No. 511, former “Lubliniak”, in flight over Hel. (Mariusz Konarski coll.)*

Lioré et Olivier LeO H-135B3

The last category of seaplanes of French manufacture used by the Polish naval aviation were the amphibious patrol and assault machines LeO H-135B3. Their construction was based on the earlier model LeO H-13B3. They differed from the original in dimensions, i.e. the fuselage was slightly longer and taller. The airframe was also heavier. What at first glance distinguished the two variants from each other was the folding wheeled landing gear, placed under the fuselage near the lower wing and lifted under the wing while the aircraft was operating from the water. The engine and armament were identical to the LeO H-13B3 model.

The Poles took over seven aircraft of this type at Vélizy-Villacoublay airfield near Paris, in the autumn of 1926. They arrived at Puck by sea in early 1927. They were incorporated into the Naval Observation Flight and the Training Section, and after the reorganization of the *MDLot.* in 1931, they were sent to the 2nd Line Flight "Rugia" *(II Eskadra Liniowa "Rugia")* and to the Training Flight. At Puck, this type of flying boat was used mainly for air training.

The construction of an amphibious airplane, equipped with a folding undercarriage, allowing also the use of land-based airfields, meant that the LeO H-135B3s were eagerly used for long-distance flights across the country.

168

[168]: The amphibious LeO H-135B3 aircraft taking off from the waters of the Bay of Puck. The lack of any markings on the nose part of the machine is noteworthy, which indicates that the photograph comes from the initial period of service with the MDLot. *(MOW in Hel)*

[169]: The LeO H-135B3 amphibian No. 66 sliding onto the water from the slipway at the MDLot. *base in Puck. The airplane sports the camouflage and marking schemes typical for French aviation. The chequerboards are painted with an inverted field layout. (MOW in Hel)*

169

170

[170]: *The LeO H-135B3 No. amphibian 66 has left the shore behind and in a moment it will launch itself into the air. In the background there is the torpedo ship ORP "Kujawiak". (MOW in Hel)*

The long-distance flights performed by the LeO H-135B3 amphibians

Date of departure	Aircraft No.	Route
February 1928	6-?	Puck – Poznań Ławica – Puck
May 1928	6-4	Puck – Bydgoszcz
May 1928	6-2	Puck – Bydgoszcz – Puck
6.02.1929	6-1	Puck – Bydgoszcz – Poznań – Zoppot
12.02.1929	6-1	Zoppot – Puck
18.02.1930	6-2	Puck – Lwów – Puck
26.08.1935	6-4	Puck – Lwów – Puck

The flight to Poznań in February 1929 was particularly memorable, when on the way back the amphibian No. 6-1 piloted by Lt. Edward Suzanowicz had to force land. This took place around 1700 hrs on the frozen waters of the Bay of Gdańsk, right next to the Sopot (Zoppot) pier, hence in the Free City of Gdańsk (Danzig) territory. As we read in the order issued by the *MDLot.* commander dated 16 February 1929:

"*... I declare for the purposes of registry and logistic that on 6.02 this year, at 1055 hrs, on seaplane No. 61 flew Lt. Suzanowicz Edward, 2nd Lt. Jesionowski Walerian and Cftsm. Zając Franciszek – destination: route Puck – Bydgoszcz – Poznań and back (order of departure No. 000774). From the above-mentioned crew, on 9.02 Lt. Majewski Zygmunt returned to the unit by rail from Poznań. During the flight Poznań – Puck on 8.02 this year, at 1700 hrs the seaplane performed a force landing in Zoppot, so the above-mentioned crew returned to the unit by rail from Zoppot, 9.02 of this year Lt. Suzanowicz Edward, on 11.02 Lt. Jesionowski Walerian, on 10.02 Cftsm. Zając Franciszek*"[1].

1 Andrzej Olejko, Lotnictwo Morskie II Rzeczypospolitej, Wyd. ZP Grupa, Warsaw, 2010, p. 149.

Four mechanics from Puck were sent to Sopot, and the repair of the damaged flying boat lasted until 12 February 1929. Then Lt. Edward Suzanowicz and 2nd Lt. Stefan Zawadzki brought it back to the base in Puck. Some sources indicated that LeO H-135B's were also used for foreign courtesy visits, but this is not true.

In spite of this, the aircraft of this type were not very popular among the personnel of the flying unit in Puck. It was difficult to pilot, not forgiving even the slightest mistakes. It was a bane for young and inexperienced pilots. This amphibian also had a tendency to tilt the wing during take-off with a side wind. In 1928–1929 alone a total of four accidents occurred, as a result of which were lost the following machines: No. 6-3 (damaged during landing on the Vistula River in Warsaw or its surroundings) as well as Nos. 6-6 and 6-7. Also damaged during take-off for a flight to Bydgoszcz was the amphibian No. 6-4, but after repairs it returned to service.

In 1930, two accidents took place that resulted in the total loss of the aircraft. The first event took place on 23 June 1930 on Lake Łapolice near Kartuzy. This basin was a reserve site for the Puck unit, and on that day three LeO H-135B3 machines took part in exercises there. After finishing the exercises, the amphibians were to return to Puck. The take-off was performed with a side wind. The first two machines took off successfully, while the third one of Lt. Siedlecki, with a crew of the 2nd Lt. Henryk Kołodziejek, Lance. Sgt. Stanisław Witas and Sgt. Maj Bolesław Rusak (mechanic), experienced problems. At an altitude of about 150 metres one of the engines' revs decreased, and the airplane went down and hit the water. The crew was in the water, after which the two remaining amphibians landed

171

[171]: *The LeO H-135B3 flying boat No. 1 (6-1) on the apron of the* MDLot. *base in Puck. The machine belongs to the 2nd Line Flight "Rugia", as evidenced by the insignia painted in the fore part of the plane. The number, reduced to the white digit "1", is painted in the centre part of the fuselage. Clearly visible are the details of the aircraft's structure – the instrument panel, machine gun turntable and engine nacelles. (Mariusz Konarski coll.)*

[172]: *The LeO H-135B3 amphibian No. 67 while moving on the water. Also this aircraft had its chequerboards painted with an inverted arrangement of squares. In the background, the port in Gdynia under construction. (NAC Archives)*

172

and the airmen were taken from the water. Seriously wounded Lt. Henryk Kołodziejek was transported to a hospital in Warsaw, the other airmen returned to Puck. Only the mechanic remained at the crash site, his task was to secure the scene of the accident in which the damaged plane was still located. It lay about 100 metres from the shoreline, in shallow waters in the rushes, and most importantly it did not sink, which gave a chance to take it ashore and transport it to Puck for refurbishment. The next day, 2nd Lt. Wiktor Złotkowski arrived at the scene, together with three NCOs and six privates from the 2nd Line Flight "Rugia" as well as two drivers from the Port Detachment. They were tasked with pulling the damaged amphibian ashore and transporting it to Puck. On the spot they found out that overnight... it had disappeared from the surface of the water. The result was a rebuke of the not guilty mechanic and an order to commence a search action. It lasted more than two weeks, the wreckage was eventually found, but it turned out that it would be necessary to use heavy equipment for its recovery. In the end only some components were collected, while the remains of the amphibian's wreck rest on the bottom of the lake to this day.

[173]: The LeO H-135B3 amphibian No. 64 at the MDLot. *base in Puck. (Wojtek Matusiak coll.)*

173

174

[174]: During the making of the film "Rhapsody of the Baltic", the aerial photographs were shot with a camera mounted on the fore machine gun post of the LeO H-135B3 No. 64. The camera itself is clearly visible in the picture. The film crew and MDLot. *officers pose in front of the airplane. (Muzeum Ziemi Puckiej)*

[175]: The LeO H-135B3 No. 61 of the 2nd Line Flight "Rugia" moored by the beach in Gdynia-Oksywie. (National Library)

175

The second crash took place in the port basin of the naval base in Gdynia-Oksywie on 28 June 1930. Aircraft No. 64 crashed into the water from a height of about 10 metres near the entrance to the port. Entangled in the steering cables, Lt. Antoni Wacięga was pulled out of the sinking airplane at the last moment by the seamen of hulk-cruiser ORP "Bałtyk". As Antoni Wacięga later recalled:

"*... It was a two-engine seaplane-amphibian LeO H, a very difficult machine that did not forgive any mistakes, and I was still a very young pilot. In the crew I was the pilot, the observer was Lieutenant Metzgier and there were two mechanics. Everyone came out intact from this overturn, and only myself had a seriously injured right leg*"[2].

On the other hand, Lt. Romuald Nałęcz-Tymiński aboard the ORP *Bałtyk* remembers this event the following way:

"*One day, while conducting classes on board, I heard a report from a signalman on watch that a seaplane was approaching from the open sea. When I approached the starboard of the ORP 'Bałtyk'; the low-level flying plane was already nearing the entrance to Gdynia's outer harbour. Having flown into the outer harbour, the plane lowered and started an approach to landing and, suddenly, with all its weight, dropped from a height of about 10 metres into the water. We ordered an "Action stations, man overboard" and we hurriedly sent a rescue team in a launch. In the cockpit sat heavily stunned Lt. Wacięga trying to get out of the increasingly submerging plane. Something, however, held him firmly by the legs. Sailors from the rescue team, having entered the fuselage, grabbed Antek's arms, but they failed to pull him from the sinking machine. Meanwhile we were running out of time. One of the rescue team – an athlete and also a footballer – having brought a naval knife, immersed himself in the confined space of the cockpit flooded with water, where he found a tangle of steel lines from the damaged fuselage, tightly wrapped around the pilot's knee. With great dedication, repeating his actions several times, at almost the last moment before the plane sank, the rescuer managed to disentangle the cables so that the sailors standing on both sides of the cockpit could take out and transfer the frazzled survivor to the motorboat. The plane disappeared under the surface of the water in a moment. The rescued Antek – we can say by a miracle – we sent it back to the Maritime Hospital, where, apart from general bruising and exhaustion, serious damage to the right knee was found. I visited Antek in the hospital in the evening, he was in a very miserable state. After recovering, Antek returned to normal service with the MDLot. Alas, his favourite sport – football – was out of question anymore*"[3].

The wounded Lt. Antoni Wacięga was taken to hospital in Warsaw, and the plane was eventually repaired, for this purpose parts from the damaged amphibian No. 67 were used.

After the events described above, only three amphibians numbered 62, 64 and 65 remained in service. In 1934, there was just one LeO H-135B3 remaining operational, it was machine No. 64. Along with the operational Schreck FBA 17 HE.2 flying boats it was assigned to the HQ Platoon. It also took part in the film "Rhapsody of the Baltic". Most of the aerial photographs of the film were shot from this aircraft, the camera was mounted to the machine gun mounting in the fore observation post. In addition, it was used to tow banners and sleeves for firing practice, also at night. In September 1936, the amphibian took part in the so-called "School of Fire" firing practice for both ground- and ship-based anti-aircraft guns. The amphibian was finally decommissioned in 1938.

2 Andrzej Olejko, Lotnictwo Morskie II Rzeczypospolitej, Wyd. ZP Grupa, Warsaw, 2010, p. 147.

3 Idem, pp. 197–198

[176]: Three amphibious LeO H-135B3 anchored on Lake Łapolice near Kartuzy during an exercise. On 23 June 1930, during a take-off, as a result of engine failure, the amphibian No. 61 crashed. The wreckage of the aircraft still rests on the bottom of the lake to this day. The photograph was taken most probably during this period. (NAC Archives)

176

Periods of service and assignments of the LeO H-135B3 amphibians

Type	No.	Delivered	Assignments within the *MDLot.*	Written off	Notes
LeO H-135B3	6-1	1927	1927 – Naval Observation Flight 1928 – Training Section 1929–1930 – Naval Observation Flight 1930 – 2nd Line Flight "Rugia"	30.07.1930	Crashed during the take-off from the Lake Łapolice near Kartuzy on 23.06.1930. The wreckage has remained on the bottom of the lake to the present.
LeO H-135B3	6-2	1927	1927–1929 – Naval Observation Flight 1929 – *MDLot.* workshops 1930 – 2nd Line Flight "Rugia"	No data available	
LeO H-135B3	6-3	1927	1927–1928 – Naval Observation Flight, 1929 – at Puck (no data on the exact assignment) 1930 – 2nd Line Flight "Rugia"	No data available	
LeO H-135B3	6-4	1927	1927–1930 – Naval Observation Flight 1930–1934 – 2nd Line Flight "Rugia" 1937–1938 – HQ Platoon	1938	
LeO H-135B3	6-5	1927	1927–1929 – Naval Observation Flight	No data available	
LeO H-135B3	6-6	1927	1927–1929 – *MDLot.'s* reserve 1930 – 2nd Line Flight "Rugia"	No data available	
LeO H-135B3	6-7	1927	1927 – *MDLot.'s* reserve	No data available	Spare parts donor

[177]: The LeO H-135B3 at the MDLot. *base in Puck. Note the lack of a number in the front part of the fuselage, which indicates the initial period of service. (MOW in Hel).*

[178]: Winter in front of the hangar at the MDLot. *base. Personnel pose for a photo at the amphibian LeO H-135B3 No. 61. The image comes from 1929, when the markings used were in the form of large white digits painted in the nose part of the aircraft. (Muzeum Ziemi Puckiej)*

179

180

[179]: *The LeO H-135B3 amphibian of the 2nd Line Flight "Rugia", Puck first half of the 1930s (Polish Aviation Museum, Kraków)*
[180]: *The machine and its crew, a LeO H-135B3 of the 2nd Line Flight "Rugia". In the background, the "Pilots' House" can be seen. (Polish Aviation Museum, Kraków)*

181

[181]: A group of the MDLot. *officers pose for a souvenir photograph in front of a LeO H-135B3. Third from the left, in a leather jacket is Lt. Adolf Stempkowski. The photo was taken in 1928 and therefore a year after the introduction of this type of aircraft into service with the* MDLot. *This is evidenced by the lack of markings in the fore part of the fuselage. (Muzeum Ziemi Puckiej)*

182

[182]: In the hangar of the base of the MDLot. *in Puck. By a LeO H-135B3 amphibian pose two officers, on the left side Lt. Adolf Stempkowski. The details of the airframe construction are clearly visible – the main undercarriage leg fixing, the step facilitating entry to the aircraft, sometimes erroneously taken for an insignia or emblem painted on the fuselage and the Venturi nozzle attached to the engine supporting strut. (Muzeum Ziemi Puckiej)*

[183]: In front of the Radio and Quality-control Section building. One of numerous commemorative photographs. Unfortunately, the officers in the image obscured the number painted on the bow of the LeO H-135B3 amphibian of the Naval Multi-Engine Flight. (MOW in Hel)

[184]: The Naval Multi-Engine Flight personnel pose for a commemorative photograph at the LeO H-135B3 amphibian No. 64. Fifth from the left in the bottom row sits Lt. Adolf Stempkowski. The circular building visible in the background accommodated the Radio and Quality-control Section. (Tomasz J. Kopański coll.)

185

[185]: The LeO H-135B3, No. 65, Naval Observation Flight (Morska Eskadra Obserwacyjna), *Puck, 1927. The aircraft is in factory finish. The upper surface in sea blue-grey* (Gris Bleu Foncé), *side surfaces of the fuselage and upper surfaces of the planes and horizontal stabilizers in light grey-blue* (Gris Bleu Clair), *the lower surfaces of the wings and the horizontal stabilizers in light grey* (Gris Clair). *The engine nacelles are in natural metal* (aluminium). *Markings in the form of white numbers not divided by a dash, painted in the nose part of the fuselage. A set of numerical and weight markings are painted on both sides of the fin.*

186

[186]: The LeO H-135B3 amphibian No. 65 (6-5) of the Naval Multi-Engine Flight sits on a transport cart in front of the Radio and Quality-control Section building at the MDLot. *base in Puck. (MOW in Hel)*

187

[187]: The LeO H-135B3, No. 3 (6-3), 2nd Line Flight (II Eskadra Liniowa) *"Rugia", Puck 1930. The aircraft in factory finish. The upper surface in sea blue-grey* (Gris Bleu Foncé), *side surfaces of the fuselage and upper surfaces of the planes and horizontal stabilizers in light grey-blue* (Gris Bleu Clair), *lower surfaces of the wings and the horizontal stabilizers in light grey* (Gris Clair). *The engine nacelles in metal natural* (aluminium). *In the nose part, the flight insignia emblem is painted on both sides, in the centre part of the fuselage there is the white figure "3". On the fin, the numerical and weight markings.*

188

[188]: The LeO H-135B3 amphibian No.3 (6-3) of the 2nd Line Flight "Rugia". Note the flight insignia painted in the fore part of the machine. Behind the front machine gun post a propeller driving the generator for the wireless set. In front of the airplane, officers and seamen of the flight are posing. (Tomasz J. Kopański coll.)

189

[189]: The LeO H-135B3, No. 2 (6-2), 2nd Line Flight (II Eskadra Liniowa) *"Rugia", Puck 1930. The aircraft is in factory finish. The upper surface in sea blue-grey* (Gris Bleu Foncé), *side surfaces of the fuselage and upper surfaces of the planes and horizontal stabilizers in light grey-blue* (Gris Bleu Clair), *the lower surfaces of the wings and the horizontal stabilizers in light grey* (Gris Clair). *The engine nacelles in natural metal* (aluminium). *Numerical and weight inscriptions visible on the fin.*

190

[190]: The LeO H-135B3 amphibian No. 6 (6-2) in all its glory. We can see all elements of the aircraft markings – the insignia of the 2nd Line Flight "Rugia" painted in the nose part of the aircraft and the aircraft number reduced only to the second digit located in the middle part of the fuselage. Note the Breguet 19 line aircraft in the background.(Stratus / zbiory W. Bączkowskiego).